United States Department of Agriculture
Forest Service

Pacific Southwest
Research Station

Research Paper
PSW-RP-264

September 2013

Pinus ponderosa: A Taxonomic Review With Five Subspecies in the United States

Robert Z. Callaham

Author

Robert Z. Callaham (retired) was a botanist and geneticist with the Pacific Southwest Research Station, 800 Buchanan Street, West Annex Building, Albany, CA 94710-0011. He served as station director from 1976 to 1983 and as de facto director of the Wildland Resources Center, University of California, from 1983 to 1990. He can be reached at rzcallaham@comcast.net.

Cover photograph: Ponderosa pine stand; photo copyright by Miles Hemstrom.

Abstract

Callaham, Robert Z. 2013. *Pinus ponderosa*: a taxonomic review with five subspecies in the United States. Res. Pap. PSW-RP-264. Albany, CA: U.S. Department of Agriculture, Forest Service, Pacific Southwest Research Station. 52 p.

Various forms of *Pinus ponderosa* Douglas ex C. Lawson are found from British Columbia southward and eastward through 16 states and, perhaps, into Mexico. The status of many names previously associated with this species, but excluded here, has been clarified. Accumulated evidence based on variation in morphology and xylem monoterpenes, partial genetic barriers to crossing, and allozyme differences leads to recognition of five subspecies:

1. *Pinus ponderosa* subsp. *ponderosa*, Columbia ponderosa pine, southward from southern British Columbia, east of the Cascade Range in Washington, Oregon, and northeastern California and eastward to the Continental Divide.
2. *Pinus ponderosa* subsp. *critchfieldiana* Callaham, subsp. nov., Pacific ponderosa pine, from Puget Sound, Washington, southward to southern California.
3. *Pinus ponderosa* subsp. *scopulorum* (Engelm. in S. Watson) E. Murray, Rocky Mountains ponderosa pine, from the Continental Divide in Montana eastward to the Black Hills of South Dakota and southward into Utah and Colorado.
4. *Pinus ponderosa* subsp. *readiana* Callaham, subsp. nov., central high plains ponderosa pine, restricted to Nebraska and adjacent areas in South Dakota, Wyoming, and Colorado.
5. *Pinus ponderosa* subsp. *brachyptera* (Engelm. in Wislizenus) Callaham, comb. nov., southwestern ponderosa pine, in Arizona, New Mexico, Oklahoma, and southwestern Texas, and, probably, extending into Mexico.

Transition zones occur between subspecies.

Keywords: Ponderosa pine, *Pinus ponderosa*, taxonomy, subspecies.

Introduction

Ponderosa pine, *Pinus ponderosa* Douglas ex C. Lawson, is a widespread species that differs substantially in morphology across its range, with resultant confusion in its taxonomy. It grows in various forms over a large area extending from British Columbia southward and eastward through 16 states.[1]

During the 1800s, separate botanical discoveries of the species in Montana, Wyoming, Colorado, Washington, California, and New Mexico resulted in it being called by different names. This confusion was compounded during the latter part of the 19th century when taxonomists included closely related species as varieties of ponderosa pine. Discoveries and taxonomy of ponderosa pine are reviewed here. A comprehensive description of the species is provided.

Since the early 1900s, ponderosa pine has been regarded as composed of two (or three) varieties or subspecies. Forestry scientists have exerted much effort to understand and utilize this genetic variability. Their studies have identified and characterized numerous geographic races and transitional zones. Five of these races are described here as subspecies (fig. 1).

Literature Review

Copies of relevant pages from historical botanical writings cited in this manuscript are in research files at the Institute of Forest Genetics, Placerville, California.

Taxonomic History

According to Sargent (1897):

> The first published allusion to *Pinus ponderosa* is in the journal of Lewis and Clark, who, in ascending the Missouri River in September, 1804, at the outset of their transcontinental journey, found the cones of this tree, brought down from the pineries of northwestern Nebraska, floating on White River, and heard of the pine forest on the Black Hills of Dakota.

Lewis and Clark's journal entry (Coues 1893, p. 117 and 150) is more ambiguous:

> September 15th. (1804) We passed, at an early hour, the creek near last night's camp; and at two mile' distance reached the mouth of White river, coming in from the south. ... the sergeant (Gass), who ascended about twelve miles; ... he saw pine burrs [sic—pine cones], and sticks of birch were seen floating down the river; ...

> October 2d. (1804) ... The Black mountains (Hills), he (Mr. Valle, a French trader) observes, are very high, covered with great quantities of pine, ...

---

[1] Ponderosa pine may extend into Mexico despite the contrary contention of Perry (1991).

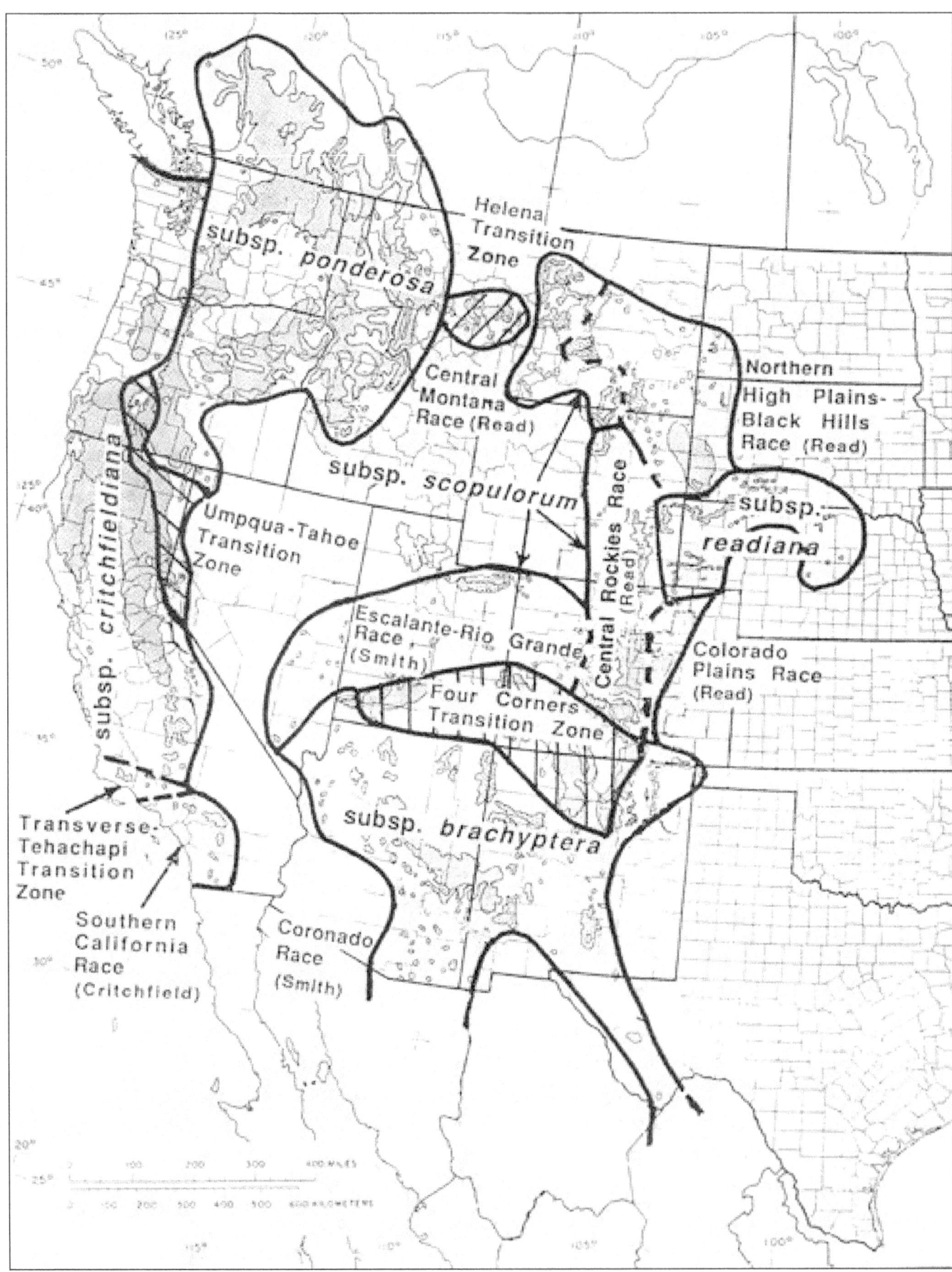

Figure 1—Location of subspecies and transition zones of ponderosa pine north of Mexico. Base map adapted from Little (1971).

Later, Lewis and Clark (Coues 1893, p. 305), when at a point now on the north shore of Fort Peck Lake, Montana, currently called "Pines Campground" and managed by the U.S. Army Corps of Engineers, wrote the first description of Rocky Mountains ponderosa pine:

> May 11th. (1805) … We saw and visited some high hills on the north side about three miles from the river, whose tops were covered with the pitch-pine. This is the first pine we have seen on the Missouri; it is like that of Virginia [*Pinus rigida* Mill.], except that the leaves are somewhat longer.

Lewis and Clark (Coues 1893, p. 318) referred again to ponderosa pine when they first viewed the large stand extending along both banks of the Missouri River at the southern boundaries of Phillips and Blaine Counties, Montana:

> May 21st. (1805). … In its course the Missouri makes a sudden and extensive bend toward the south, to receive the waters of the Muscleshell. … The country on the south is high, broken, and crowned with some pine and dwarf cedar; the leaf of this pine is longer than that of the common pitch or red pine of Virginia [*Pinus rigida*]; the cone is longer and narrower, the imbrications are wider and thicker, and the whole is frequently covered with rosin.

Lauria (1996) wrote:

Pinus ponderosa s.l. is a commercially important and polymorphic conifer. Its taxonomy (and that of its entire group, the "ponderosa complex") is far from being settled. This unsettled status is largely due to absence of a type, a circumstance that also accounts for the fact that even the very identity of *Pinus ponderosa s.str.* itself is notoriously confused. The earliest sources documenting the intricacies of the discovery and late publication of ponderosa pine as a new species in 1836 were reviewed. Detailed study of its earliest botanical history is demonstrated to be essential to finally establish its original identity, as meant by David Douglas and described by Charles Lawson. *Pinus ponderosa* Douglas ex C. Lawson is then neotypified with authentic material (an ovuliferous cone) discovered in a historical collection of conifer cones surviving at the Natural History Museum in Vienna, Austria (W). The extensive synonymy pertaining to the "ponderosa complex" is reviewed (including typification of several of these synonyms) and some new facets of the life and achievements of David Douglas, who is commonly credited with the discovery of *Pinus ponderosa*, are also reported here for the first time.

Further, according to Lauria:[2] foliage specimens of *Pinus ponderosa* collected by Lewis and Clark were mounted (in about 1810) by Frederick Pursh, were rediscovered in 1897 by Thomas Meehan, and are:

"...in the custody of the Academy of Natural Sciences in Philadelphia."

Lewis' original annotations on the specimens, having in most cases been made on paper of poor quality, are not preserved. But Pursh as a rule transcribed Lewis' annotations correctly, although not necessarily verbatim. On both of the sheets of Lewis' ponderosa pine preserved today, the labels deviate only little in content:

On the Kooskooskee / On River bottoms, in / rich land, west of the / mountains. / Octbr. 1st 1805. The specimens only consist of sterile parts; reproductive parts are neither present today nor is their former existence documented anywhere.

Because the material was destitute of cones, and because Lewis used the name "long-leafed pine" on several occasions in his journal, what other choice would any herbarium taxonomist (like Pursh in 1814!) have but to identify this material as *P. palustris*?—the collection by Lewis and Clark had been identified erroneously as *Pinus palustris* L. by F. Pursh.

Lauria commented further: "The chronologically next allusion to *P. ponderosa* is that of Edwin James (1823, 1825) who erroneously identified it as *Pinus resinosa* (without author!) in 1820."

Edwin P. James (1825), Assistant Surgeon, U.S. Army, described and catalogued plants collected during the expedition to the Rocky Mountains commanded by Major Stephen H. Long. James was taken on the expedition specifically to serve as botanist and geologist. James erroneously identified, as *Pinus resinosa*, ponderosa pines that he encountered on Platte River, Wyoming, and Pikes Peak, Colorado, and probably elsewhere in the Rocky Mountains and adjacent high plains.

According to Goodman:[3]

James mentioned *Pinus resinosa* in his diary on July 10 (erroneously as July 11) [1820]. He very possibly had seen this pine the day before in Douglas County Colorado and certainly had seen it from Elephant Rock (his Castle Rock) to his campsite near the Air Force Academy, El Paso County.

James failed to collect any specimens for identification by others.

---

[2] Lauria, F. 1995. Personal communication. Naturhistorische Museum Wien, Vienna, Austria.
[3] Goodman, G.J. 1996. Personal communication. Department of Botany and Microbiology, University of Oklahoma, Norman, Oklahoma.

Returning to Lauria's explanations:

When John Torrey (1828) determined and listed some of the plants already reported by James, it was not he who misapplied *Pinus resinosa* for *P. ponderosa*. In the absence of any material, he had to rely on James' published account (1823) and on his list of plants (1825). However, Torrey's repetition of "*Pinus resinosa*" misapplied for *Pinus ponderosa* is at the origin of *Pinus resinosa* Torrey, reported as a synonym of *P. ponderosa* by G.B. Sudworth (1897) and C.S. Sargent (1898).

David Douglas repeatedly made the same mistake in the Pacific Northwest. In "An account of a new species of *Pinus* (*lambertiana* Dougl.), native of California," Douglas (1827) wrote:

The trees do not form dense forests as most of the other Pines which clothe the face of North-west America, but like *Pinus resinosa* (actually *P. ponderosa*), which grows among them, they are scattered singly over the plains...

In the first publication of extracts of his journal of travels (1836: 108), he wrote on April 19, 1826: while traveling by boat up the Columbia River:

Many kinds of Pine are seen on the banks, three species particularly,— *P. resinosa* (actually *P. ponderosa*), a *Pinus*, very similar to *P. taxifolia* [actually *Pseudotsuga menziesii* (Mirb.) Franco] of the coast, and *P. Larix* (actually *Larix occidentalis* Nutt.), ...

His first collection of ponderosa pine (as host of a new mistletoe, or *Arceuthobium*) also was misidentified in the field as *Pinus resinosa*; the time was either 11th or 12th of May, 1826; the place was "the old Establishment" on the "Spokan (sic) River," presumably near what is now Spokane, Washington.

Lauria deduced that after returning to London:

... between April and July 1829 ... Douglas concluded he had a new pine among his specimens and coined for it the name *Pinus ponderosa*. Also at this stage he must have converted his annotation *Pinus resinosa* to *Pinus ponderosa* on his herbarium-sheet of *Arceuthobium*.

At that time, Douglas must also have converted the record in his journal entry of May 1826, for it reads: 'I also saw a new *Pinus* (*P. ponderosa*) and two kinds of *Misseltoe* (sic), one large and growing on this Pine; ...' (Douglas 1836: 111). This then is the source of the specific epithet *Pinus ponderosa*, named for its heavy wood. Douglas never described the foliage, immature cone, or seeds that he carried back to Edinburgh, Scotland.

Loudon (1830: 387) listed the species, credited its name to Douglas in 1828 (not 1826), but also failed to describe it.

The first valid description of *Pinus ponderosa* dates from the scanty English-language characterization, by a Scottish nurseryman, Charles Lawson, in Lawson and Son (1836). Described is an 8-year-old tree, lacking cones, grown from Douglas' seed, which Lauria[4] notes had been sown in gardens of the Horticultural Society of London.

Lawson did not designate a holotype. Probably following Louden, he attributed the species to David Douglas in 1828. Therefore, *Pinus ponderosa* Douglas ex C. Lawson (1836) is the correct name and citation.

The publication in which the description appears could be attributed to "Peter Lawson and Son" (1836) if only knowledge internal to that document were considered. I have accepted Lauria's[5] recommendation that the authority for this name should be C. Lawson based on Lauria's external knowledge:

> After the death of Peter Lawson in 1820 (years before Douglas' trip to collect in North America), the firm continued to be called Peter Lawson and Son, but was exclusively run by Charles Lawson. "Agriculturists Manual" was issued by the firm with its composite name, but the author was clearly Charles Lawson alone. ...

According to Lauria (who made a fruitless search in the United Kingdom in 1992), there is neither a holotype nor any other specimen for *Pinus ponderosa*:

> The tree from which Lawson's description was made no longer exists, and a search of all possibly relevant herbaria (BM, CGE, E, K, OXF) (sic) revealed no herbarium material from it, so no lectotype can be chosen. A correct typification therefore requires the determination of the origin of Douglas' seeds from which also Lawson's tree was grown. Douglas was not very informative in this respect, but does state that he did not personally collect it (Douglas 1914: 205). ... In conclusion, John Work ... a traveling trader for the Hudson Bay Company ... may have collected the requested seeds of *Pinus ponderosa* somewhere on Pend Oreille River, or he may have returned in time to collect them at Kettle Falls, or possibly elsewhere on his travels.

> It is not now possible to determine where from historical evidence. ... Douglas met John Work again at Kettle Falls in April 1827 on his return trip overland to Hudson Bay (Douglas 1914: 246) and it is presumed here

---

[4] See footnote 2.

[5] See footnote 2.

that Work on this occasion handed over to Douglas the seeds he was able to gather in October of the previous year. However, it is certain that Douglas, on his return in October 1827, among other species also brought to Britain seeds of *Pinus ponderosa* ... .

A number of the trees grown from this seed still survive in British arboreta... . These are of course of the same seed lot from which Lawson described his tree, and so botanically closely comparable. Most of these trees were studied by the author (Lauria) in spring 1992; they all appear to be quite homogeneous in their botanical characters, and will presumably have shared these traits with Lawson's tree. This finally enables the determination of the true identity of *Pinus ponderosa*, as meant by Douglas and defined by Lawson, ... also allowing the designation of a neotype.

Specific and Varietal Epithets

Descriptions under several specific and varietal epithets attest to the geographic diversity of ponderosa pine. On August 24, 1846, Hartweg (1847) discovered a luxuriant form, growing in a very small stand at what now is called Bonny Doon, just north of Santa Cruz, California. Hartweg (1848p. 221, 223, 225) later found the same pine in foothills of Sierra Nevada along Bear Creek (now Bear River, east of Wheatland, California). His published description was under the name *Pinus benthamiana* Hart. Both Vasey (1876) and Lemmon (1888) considered this form to be *P. ponderosa* var. *benthamiana* (Hart.) Vasey. Trees growing at Bonny Doon were studied by Callaham (2013) and found to be indistinguishable taxonomically from other Pacific ponderosa pines, growing from southern California northward through western Oregon to Puget Sound.

Andrew Murray (1855) described two new species, *Pinus beardsleyi* A. Murr. and *Pinus craigana* A. Murr., from two collections made by his brother William Murray. The collections were separated by 1,000 feet of elevation, near the top of a mountain[6] at about 41° N in northern California. He noted that his two new species "seem to have more affinity with *P. Benthamiana* than any other described species."

Lauria, in 1992, searched for, but did not find at either Kew or Edinburgh, surviving type specimens from these two collections; his search disclosed that George Engelmann, in 1869, had acquired material from these collections and

---

[6] See 2. According to Lauria, the location was Scott Mountain, approximately 39°39' N, longitude 122° 37' 42" W. The summit, at 6,829 feet elevation, is the meeting point of not only Siskiyou, Trinity, and Shasta Counties, but also of Klamath, Trinity, and Shasta National Forests.

"... identified the material of both of these specimens (sterile shoots) as belonging to *Pinus ponderosa*."[7] In fact, this material merely is representative of morphological variability found either among individual trees within a stand or associated with elevational change (Callaham and Liddicoet 1961, Conkle 1973).

Lemmon (1889) designated darker, young, rapid-growing populations of this form, growing in the very best sites of the Sierra Nevada, as *P. ponderosa* var. *nigricans* Lemmon. He wrote: "This form is generally found in company with the larger, typical, whitish-barked trees, but in moister localities." He failed to recognize that these "black-Jacks" (a term used by loggers) were merely younger trees (probably second-growth following widespread cutting during California's Gold Rush) that would mature into the large old trees with yellowish-tan plated bark found in the Sierra Nevada.

Wislizenus (1848, p. 17), on June 25, 1846, on the Santa Fe Trail in New Mexico, reported a new variety of what is now ponderosa pine (McKelvey 1955). He first found it on the east side of Sangre de Cristo Mountains, along Gallinas Creek, south of Las Vegas en route to a campsite, probably now Romeroville.[8] [9] Dr. Wislizenus noted on the type specimen at Missouri Botanical Garden, "The most common pine ... begin about Rock creek (*sic*) to Santa Fe."

Engelmann (1848) described his specimens as *Pinus brachyptera* Engelm. Lemmon (1888) reducing this species to *P. ponderosa* var. *brachyptera* (Engelm.) wrote: "This pine was so named by Dr. Engelmann, from a mistaken impression that the seed wings were very short." [However, it was Lemmon, not Engelmann, who erred, for this taxon does have very short seed wings (Callaham 2013)]. Two names, *Pinus brachyptera* Engelm. (1848) and *P. ponderosa* var. *brachyptera* (Engelm.) Lemmon (1888), were applied briefly to the form found on the high plateau of northern Arizona and New Mexico and probably extending southward into the northern states of Mexico. However, for most of the 20th century, trees growing in the Southwest have been called *P. ponderosa* var. *scopulorum*.

Engelmann (1879) [1880] designated "*P. ponderosa* of the Rocky Mountain floras" as *P. ponderosa* var. *scopulorum* Engelm. in a book by Sereno Watson. Lemmon (1897) elevated this variety to *Pinus scopulorum* (Engelm.) Lemmon. Edward Murray (1982), a century later, elevated Engelmann's variety to a subspecies.

---

[7] Attachment, dated August 1992, to personal communication from Friedrich Lauria, Naturhistorische Museum Wien, Vienna, Austria, February 28, 1994.

[8] Salazar, R.J. 1991. Personal communication. Chief, Archival Services, State Records Center and Archives, Santa Fe, NM.

[9] Read, R.A. 1992. Personal communication. Read stated that his sample number 864 was from Romeroville, the site of the original discovery by Wislizenus.

Lauria (1991), an authority on *Pinus* subsect. *Ponderosae*, was distraught over:

> ... inconsistencies between the vast amount of data already available on the group and its present taxonomic arrangement. By and by it becomes apparent that a variety of profound misconceptions deeply rooted in the minds of modern researchers in this particular field is responsible for the fact that the pattern of variability and diversity is still poorly understood in *Pinus ponderosa*, in the *Ponderosa–complex*, and in the *Ponderosae* in general... . (p. 137) The controversy on the geographic origin of *Pinus ponderosa* as a whole perhaps also illustrates that *Pinus ponderosa sensu lato* of the Pacific Northwest appears yet not to have been adequately surveyed botanically, and that this "race" [Weidman's (1939) north plateau called Columbia here] and Sierra Nevada western slope ponderosa pine, in fact represent entirely different things, actually entities too different in several respects, and the northern race itself too incoherent a group, to be termed "races" of only a single taxon.

Lauria (1996) lamented the need for a taxonomic review of *Pinus ponderosa sensu lato*. The study reported here is thought to fulfill his desire for a comprehensive, range-wide review of the species, but admittedly only of its range north of Mexico.

Washoe Pine

Washoe pine and its relationship to ponderosa pine require special attention here. Geneticists at the Institute of Forest Genetics (IFG), Placerville, California, found and sampled a unique population of ponderosa pine growing at very high elevation, just east of the summit of Mount Rose, north of Lake Tahoe, Nevada. It differed from nearby Pacific ponderosa pine by its very small, ovoid cones and short, thick needles. After the director of IFG, Palmer Stockwell, showed the population to Professor Herbert Mason, University of California, Mason decided its differences from ponderosa pine warranted its designation as *Pinus washoensis* H. Mason & Stockw. (Mason and Stockwell 1945).

Haller (1961) reported Washoe pine from the Warner Mountains in northeastern California and described Washoe pine as a "probable introgressant of *Pinus ponderosa* in northeastern California ..."

After studying Washoe pine in California and Oregon, Haller (1965) wrote: "In view of the morphological continuum between *P. ponderosa* and *P. washoensis* in many localities, the status of the latter as a species seems questionable."

Ting (1966) described Washoe pine as a variety of ponderosa pine. Murray (1982) arbitrarily elevated Ting's variety to the rank of subspecies.

Smith (1967, 1971) concluded, based on monoterpenes in xylem oleoresin, that Washoe pine may be most closely related to Rocky Mountains ponderosa pine, which he later found to be chemically indistinguishable from Columbia ponderosa pine (Smith 1977).

Critchfield (1984) drew three conclusions: Washoe pine crosses freely with Rocky Mountains ponderosa pine; it is morphologically distinct and partially isolated genetically from Pacific ponderosa pine; it most resembles and may be a late pleistocene offshoot of Columbia ponderosa pine.

Lauria (1997), from his scholarly study of its taxonomic status, concluded: "*Pinus washoensis* ... was found to be identical (conspecific) with *P. ponderosa* ... 'North Plateau race' of *P. ponderosa* var. *ponderosa*."

Brayshaw (1997) described Washoe and ponderosa pines as he found them on Promontory Hill near Merritt, British Columbia, Canada.

Rehfeldt (1999a) concluded that Washoe pine and North Plateau race (Columbia ponderosa pine) were synonymous.

Excluded Taxa

Several taxa in genus *Pinus* now regarded as distinct species sometimes have been united with ponderosa pine. Taxa hereby excluded from *Pinus ponderosa* are as follows:

- *Pinus apacheca* Lemmon, Erythea 2:103, t. 3. 1894.—syn. of *P. ponderosa* *fide* G.R. Shaw 1914. = *Pinus engelmannii* Carrière *fide* Critchfield and Little (1966), Little (1979).

- *Pinus arizonica* Engelmann (1878) in Wheeler, Rpt. U.S. Geogr. Surv. 6: 260.—syn. of *P. ponderosa* *fide* G.R. Shaw (1909, 1914).—Type: Arizona, Santa Rita Mountains, 7,000 feet, 1874. *J.F. Rothrock*, 652 (holotype: MO, 3377654). Accepted as *Pinus arizonica* by Lemmon (1889), C. Sargent (1898), Peloquin (1984), Conkle and Critchfield (1988), and Rehfeldt (1993).

- *Pinus deflexa* Torrey in Emory, Rpt. U.S. Mex. Boundary Surv. 2:1, 209, t. 56. 1859.—syn. of *P. ponderosa* *fide* G.R. Shaw (1914). = *Pinus jeffreyi* var. *deflexa* (Torrey) Lemmon, Rpt. Calif. St. Bd. Forestry, 74 (1888). Described by Lemmon as "In the Sierra and southward at usually higher altitues (*sic*), often very large trees. Timber less sappy. Bark reddish. Yearling cones purple."

- *Pinus engelmannii* Carrière, Rev. Hort. 4(3): 227. 1854. "*engelmanni*." (A renaming of *P. macrophylla* Engelm. 1848, not *P. macrophylla* Lindley 1839.)—syn. of *P. ponderosa* *fide* G.R. Shaw (1914). Accepted as *Pinus engelmannii* Carrière by Critchfield and Little (1966), Little (1979).

- *Pinus jeffreyi* Grev. & Balf. in A. Murray (often cited as "Oregon Committee"), Bot. Exped. Oregon [Rpt. 8] 2, pl. 1853.—syn. of *P.*

ponderosa fide G.R. Shaw (1914). Accepted as *Pinus jeffreyi* by Lemmon (1888), Sudworth (1897), Mirov (1929), Righter and Duffield (1951), Duffield (1952), Haller (1962), Critchfield and Little (1966), and Little (1979)].

- *Pinus jeffreyi* var. *ambigua* Lemmon, Bull. Calif. State Board For. 7:11. 1889—*P. jeffreyi* var. *montana*. Lemmon (1895), Handb. West-Amer. Cone-Bearers, ed. 3, 35, *nom. superfl., illegit.*—syn. of *P. ponderosa fide* Sudworth (1897). = *Pinus ponderosa fide* C. Sargent 1898. Lemmon (1889) wrote: "A pine noted by Canby and Sargent, in Flathead Lake Valley, Montana, as being 'the prevailing tree of the valley, with purple cones, and long glaucous foliage.' This tree probably belongs with the *jeffreyi* group of forms, although Professor Sargent doubtfully referred it to *P. ponderosa* in his report of 'Forest Trees of America,' in the 10th United States Census, page 193, 1884." *Pinus jeffreyi* does not occur in Montana *fide* Critchfield and Little (1966). The study reported by Callaham (2013) included a plot at the north end of Flathead Lake Valley, and trees from that plot were typical of *P. ponderosa* subsp. *ponderosa*.
- *Pinus latifolia* Sargent, Garden and Forest 2: 496, pl. 135. 1889 (sometimes cited as *P. latifolia* Mayr[10]).—syn. of *P. ponderosa fide* G.R. Shaw (1914). = *Pinus engelmannii* Carrière *fide* Lemmon (1893) and Critchfield and Little (1966), Little (1979).
- *Pinus macrophylla* Engelm. in Wislizenus, Mem. Tour No. Mex. (Senate Misc. Publ. 26, 30th U.S. Congress) 103, 1848, not Lindley 1839 = *Pinus engelmannii* Carrière.
- *Pinus mayriana* Sudworth, Bulletin of the U.S. Department of Agriculture Division of Forestry 14:21. 1897.—syn. of *P. ponderosa fide* G.R. Shaw (1914) = *Pinus engelmannii* Carrière (see *P. ponderosa* var. *mayriana* below).
- *Pinus nootkatensis* Hort. ex Manetti (1844), *nomen nudum*, Caesarei Regii Horti Modiciam, Sup. Primum, Mediolani 28.—syn. of *P. ponderosa fide* Gordon (1862) and Sudworth (1897).
- *Pinus parryana* Gordon (1858), Pinet. 202, not Engelm.—syn. of *P. ponderosa fide* G.R. Shaw (1914). = *Pinus attenuata* Lemmon.
- *Pinus peninsularis* Lemmon, W. Amer. Conebear. 114. 1900.— syn. of *P. ponderosa fide* G.R. Shaw (1914). Duffield and Cumming (1949) failed to find *Pinus ponderosa* in Baja California. = *Pinus jeffreyi* var. *peninsularis* Lemmon (1888). Cited by Lemmon as "On the highest central range of mountains in the Peninsula of Lower California."

---

[10] See footnote 2.

- *Pinus ponderosa* var. *arizonica* (Engelm. in Wheeler) G.R. Shaw, Pines Mex., Publ. Arnold Arbor. 1, 24, pl. 17, figs. 4–5. 1909. = *Pinus arizonica* Engelm. in Wheeler (see *Pinus arizonica* above).

- *Pinus ponderosa* subsp. *arizonica* (Engelm. in Wheeler) E. Murray, Kalmia 12:23. 1982. = *Pinus arizonica* (see *Pinus arizonica* above).

- *Pinus ponderosa* subsp. *coulteri* (D. Don) E. Murray, Kalmia 12:23. 1982. = *Pinus coulteri* D. Don [*cf.*, G.R. Shaw (1914), Righter and Duffield (1951), Duffield (1952), Critchfield and Little (1966), Little and Critchfield (1969), Little (1979), Index Kewensis, Supl. XVIII, 244. 1987].

- *Pinus ponderosa* var. *jeffreyi* (Grev. & Balf. in A. Murray) Vasey, Catalogue of Forest Trees, U.S. Government Printing Office. 30. 1876. = *Pinus jeffreyi* (see *Pinus jeffreyi* above).

- *Pinus ponderosa* subsp. *jeffreyi* (Grev. & Balf. in A. Murray) E. Murray, Kalmia 12: 23. 1982. = *Pinus jeffreyi* (see *Pinus jeffreyi* above).

- *Pinus ponderosa* var. *macrophylla* (Engelm.) G.R. Shaw, Pines Mex. Publ. Arnold Arb. 1, 24, pl. 17, figs. 2–3, 6. 1909,—based on *Pinus macrophylla* (see above). = *Pinus engelmannii* Carrière.

- *Pinus ponderosa* var. *mayriana* (Sudworth) Sargent, Silva No. Amer. 11:81. 1898—syn. of *Pinus latifolia fide* C. Sargent (1889) and of *Pinus mayriana fide* Sudworth (1897)—According to Sargent (1898), this variety (or species) is based on a collection from an isolated single tree growing at lower elevation than typical southwestern ponderosa pine on the southern slopes of the Santa Rita Mountains in southeastern Arizona. = *Pinus engelmannii* Carrière *fide* Lemmon (1893).

- *Pinus ponderosa* var. *stormiae* (Martinez) Silba, Phytologia 68: 59. 1990. Silba transferred *Pinus arizonica* var. *stormiae* Martinez to *Pinus ponderosa* and suggested that it may be distributed "possibly also in Chisos Mountains, Texas, United States." Trees having three to five needles per fascicle have been observed in the Chisos Mountains by Little.[11] Specimens from one plot in the Chisos Mountains, collected for the study reported by Callaham (2013), were typical of *P. ponderosa* subsp. *brachyptera*. Consideration of the variation in ponderosa pine that may exist in Mexico is beyond the scope of this paper. Furthermore, Silba's description of his taxon indicates to me that it should not be included under *Pinus ponderosa* because needles are in fascicles of 3 to 5, not 3 as in southwestern ponderosa pine, and female cones are (1) too long, (2) curved rather than either

---

[11] Little, E.L., Jr. 1998. Personal communication. Dendrologist, retired, U.S. Department of Agriculture, Forest Service, Washington, DC.

straight or only slightly curved, and (3) persistent rather than deciduous during the first winter after ripening.

- *Pinus sinclairii* Hooker & Arnott, Bot. Beechey Voy. 392, t. 93. London, 1840.—(according to Lauria,[12] sometimes written as *sinclaireana* and *sinclairiana* Carrière, Traité Gén. Conif. Paris, 1855, 355)—syn. of *P. ponderosa fide* Sudworth 1897. = *Pinus radiata* D. Don fide C. Sargent (1898).

Genetic Investigations

Foresters and forest geneticists have grown and compared ponderosa pines collected from different provenances in "common garden" plantings since 1910 (Wang 1977). Only their findings related to differentiation of races of ponderosa pine are discussed here.

Kempff (1928) from 11- to 17-year-old plantings near Priest River, Idaho, found: (*using names defined herein*) Pacific (Mount Shasta) source had no resistance to deep continental frost; North Plateau race was superior to Rocky Mountains race; Rocky Mountains race was superior to Southwestern race.

Larson (1967) studied responses of 6-weeks-old ponderosa pine seedlings from southwestern (Coconino National Forest), Pacific (Angeles National Forest, Critchfield's Southern California race), and Rocky Mountains (Black Hills) races. Seedlings were grown under combinations of constant air and soil temperatures and combinations of day and night temperatures. Root growth responded more to soil temperature. Top growth responded more to air temperature. Epicotyl length, root penetration, number of lateral roots, and dry weight of roots were correlated with daily degree hours of each treatment. Source of seed had a pronounced effect on final seedling size. Pacific seedlings were largest. Black Hills seedlings were smallest.

LaFarge (1977) measured stem taper in Wells' 10-year-old ponderosa pine plantation in Michigan. He found that Pacific ponderosa pines were more cylindrical (less taper) vs. more conical *ponderosa* var. *scopulorum* (more taper).

Moore and Kidd (1982) studied germination under induced moisture stress using seeds collected from 76 ponderosa pines from 11 seed zones throughout Colorado. They concluded that two seed zones in the dry plains and foothills east of the Front Range (central high plains race) were adapted to more xeric conditions. Sources adapted to the most mesic conditions represented seed zones in the southwest part of Colorado (Four Corners transition zone, strongly influenced by summer monsoonal precipitation). The remaining seed sources represented seed zones in the central, mountainous part of Colorado (Rocky Mountains race).

---

[12] See footnote 2.

Read (1980, 1983) studied 24 characteristics of seedlings (grown 3 years near Hastings, Nebraska) from 80 ponderosa pines growing in the Great Plains and adjacent Rocky Mountain states. Thirteen traits provided a basis for grouping into nine geographical clusters. Two of his clusters, California and the North Plateau (Oregon, Washington, Idaho, and western Montana) fit the description of *Pinus ponderosa* var. *ponderosa*. Other clusters, east of the Continental Divide and including one Arizona source west of that divide, were described as *P. ponderosa* var. *scopulorum* and divided into: (1) Transition between the two varieties in west-central Montana, (2) Central Montana, (3) Central Rockies from north-central Wyoming to south-central Colorado, (4) Black Hills and surrounding High Plains from eastern Montana to western Nebraska, (5) Easternmost low altitude in northern Nebraska, (6) Colorado Plains east of the Front Range, and (7) Southern Rockies from extreme southern Colorado through central New Mexico and Arizona.

Read (1983) reported on attributes of his 10-year-old progenies planted near Hastings, Nebraska. Read and Sprackling (1981), in Read's 13-year-old planting, observed that North Plateau and southwestern races suffered very heavy damage by marble-sized hail. Rocky Mountains and central High Plains sources suffered only moderate to light damage. Van Haverbake (1988) reported 15-year results of Read's study.

Conkle and Critchfield (1988)—after summarizing information on geographic distribution of the species and inherent variation associated with geography—recognized two varieties, six geographic races, five ecotypes, or seven to nine statistically derived geographical clusters. They covered variation in:

- Morphology, both *in situ* and that expressed in "common garden" plantings.
- Monoterpenes in the turpentine fraction of oleoresin exuded from xylem.
- Allozymes.

Most importantly, they summarized attempts to hybridize ponderosa pine that identified both its genetic isolation from related species and genetic isolation among its races.

Earlier, Critchfield (1984) summarized what was known about genetic barriers to crossing within the species. However, he adequately tested crossability for only one of ten possible interracial crosses.

He found genetic barriers that limited crosses between Pacific and Rocky Mountains races to 35 percent. Crossability from his few crosses between Pacific and North Plateau races appeared on the order of 50 percent. He also concluded there was no evidence for phylogenetic affinity between southwestern and Pacific races. He was first to map races and transition zones as were delineated by Callaham (2013).

Linhart et al. (1989) studied allozymes from a small number of individuals resulting from Pacific x Pacific and Pacific x Rocky Mountains parents. Niebling and Conkle (1990) surveyed allozyme variation to determine the relationship between Pacific race and Washoe pine, the latter considered here to be synonymous with Columbia race. The overall conclusion was that Rocky Mountains race differed significantly from both the Pacific race and Columbia race.

Smith (1981) was first to establish the importance of color of immature cones for identifying typical ponderosa pine of the Columbia basin from other varieties or races—it being red to purple and all others being green to yellow-green.

Rehfeldt (1986a, 1986b, 1990, 1991, 1993) studied 353 seedling progenies, representing populations of ponderosa pines along a broad transect from Canada to Mexico. His comprehensive and important provenance studies—almost entirely of non-taxonomic characters—demonstrated:

- Patterns of variation within races of ponderosa pine were continuous and clinal.
- These patterns repeated among races as latitude, longitude, and elevation changed.

Finding clinal patterns of variation, sometimes very steep, wherever he looked within ponderosa pine, he ignored the existence of subspecific taxa within this complex species. He was frustrated that taxonomists were unable, some unwilling, to recognize the importance of elevational patterns of variability. Suspecting they simply did not know how to treat it; he wrote:

> ...enormous differences, both genetic and phenotypic, separate geographically distant populations, and, therefore, it is useful to have a name available; perhaps a map without lines on it would be more descriptive of the actual situation.[13]

Being fully sympathetic with Rehfeldt's viewpoints, I also recognize the necessity of placing lines or shaded bands, demarking taxa, on maps where they are warranted by significant variation in taxonomic characters.

Rehfeldt et al. (1996) and Rehfeldt (1999b) reported on cones and foliage from 295 trees of *Ponderosae* taxa in Arizona, New Mexico, and Texas. What they and he classified and labeled as *Pinus ponderosa* var. *scopulorum* was synonymous with southwestern ponderosa pine as described and labeled herein.

---

[13] Rehfeldt, G. 1998. Personal communication. Geneticist, U.S. Department of Agriculture, Forest Service, Intermountain Research Station, Moscow, ID.

Smith (1977) recognized and mapped, within ponderosa pine, five regions and four transition zones based on frequency of five major monoterpenes found in xylem oleoresin. He proposed and established through further research:[14]

Absence or relative amount of each of these monoterpenes is controlled by a single gene with two additive alleles at the locus. The relative level of a monoterpene found in a population then depends upon the frequency of two alleles within that population.

Smith (1977) presented evidence for a southern California race (his San Jacinto Region) south of his narrow transition zone in the Transverse Range and Tehachapi Mountains. Smith divided Critchfield's southwestern ponderosa pine into two regions and a transition zone.

Smith found no chemical evidence for subdividing Rocky Mountains ponderosa pine or for distinguishing it from typical Columbia ponderosa pine. However, after plotting Smith's data, Read[15] found slight but recognizable differences in proportion of *beta*-pinene in monoterpenes between Rocky Mountains ponderosa pine (21 to 28 percent) and Columbia ponderosa pine (14 to 22 percent).

Prompted by Read's finding, Callaham (2013) reexamined Smith's data and found that northern Rocky Mountains ponderosa pine differed significantly from Columbia ponderosa pine, growing to the west, by having more *alpha*-pinene, more *beta*-pinene, less *delta*-3-carene, and less myrcene. Western Rocky Mountains ponderosa pine (in Utah and Nevada) differed from Columbia ponderosa pine, growing to the north, by having more *alpha*-pinene, less *delta*-3-carene, and less myrcene.

Rotach in his unpublished doctoral dissertation (Swiss Federal Institute of Technology, Zurich, 1997) came to the conclusion that Critchfield's demarcation line along the Cascade crest was unwarranted and that "purported" races on both sides of the crest had the same evolutionary history. He studied patterns of genetic variation in allozymes and seedling quantitative traits.

Sorenson et al. (2001) studied patterns of adaptive variation within and between two parapatric races of ponderosa pine (Pacific and North Plateau) in southern Oregon.

(Their) data supported a narrow, adaptive transition for a complex of traits related to cold hardiness and provided evidence that plant vigor traits were more closely adapted to environments in the North Plateau than in the Pacific region.

---

[14] Smith, R.H. 1995. Personal communication. Retired entomologist, U.S. Department of Agriculture, Forest Service, Intermountain Research Station, Moscow, ID.

[15] Personal communication to W.B. Critchfield, September 21, 1982.

Haller and Vivrette (2011) assigned a new varietal name *pacifica* Haller to the Pacific race of ponderosa pine.

Callaham (2013) identified five distinct races and intervening transition zones of ponderosa pine in geographic regions. Samples for study were collected from plots located at elevational intervals along latitudinal transects (fig. 2). Data included:

- Fifteen characteristics of branches and foliage from 10 or fewer trees on 147 plots.
- Three characteristics of cones from 120 of those plots
- Seven characteristics of seeds from 78 of those plots.

Callaham also collected data on foliage and branch characteristics from three common-garden plantings of 10 widespread provenances. Characteristics found to be useful discriminators among Callaham's five races included:

- Branches per whorl
- Foliated length of branch
- Length and thickness of needles
- Proportional length of needle fascicles
- Number of needles per fascicle
- Number of hypodermal cell layers in corners of needles
- Number of adaxial resin ducts in needles
- Cone form
- Seed form
- Length of seed wing

Needle length was picked as a discriminator of all races. Number of hypodermal cell layers was picked in four of five comparisons. Needle thickness was a discriminator in two of five comparisons. All characteristics used to discriminate races exhibited significant inherent variation associated with provenance. Only branch angle discriminated the Pacific race from the Southwestern race.

Data from Weidman's (1939) provenance study showed that needle length, needle thickness, and number of hypodermal cell layers were under strongest genetic control. Substantial differences among races were deemed to warrant their being given separate taxonomic identities.

Implications for Taxonomy

The magnitude and significance of inherent patterns of variation within ponderosa pine provide bases for decisions about infraspecific taxonomy. Designation of five subspecies within ponderosa pine is supported primarily by previously cited findings of inherent variation in morphology and xylem monoterpenes, and to a

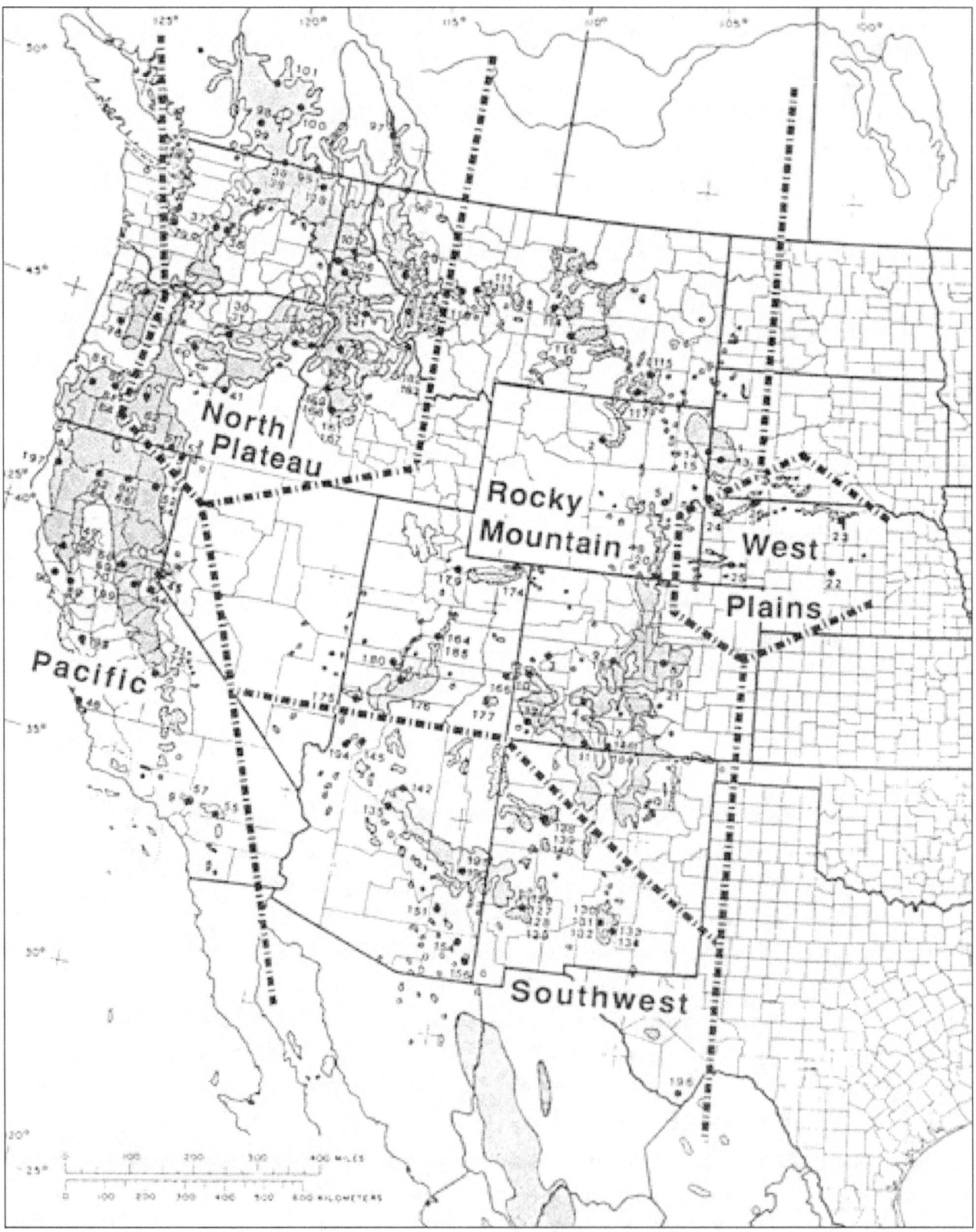

Figure 2—Distribution of ponderosa pine and 147 plots established for Callaham's (2013) rangewide study.

lesser extent by evidence of partial genetic barriers to crossing and of differences in allozymes among three subspecies.

The following text starts with ponderosa pine's taxonomy and a general description of characteristics of the species. Taxonomy—including type specimens, attributable synonyms, cultivars, and sports—is followed by description of morphological and monoterpene characters with contrasts in characters among subspecies. Successive sections of the text treat each of five subspecies in a parallel manner.

- *Pinus ponderosa* Douglas ex C. Lawson, Agriculturist's Manual p. 354. 1836.—*Pinus ponderosa* Douglas ex Loud., Hort. Brit. p. 387. 1830, *nomen nudum,*—*Pinus ponderosa* Douglas, Companion Bot. Mag. 2:111, 141. 1836, *nomen nudum.* Type unknown, see neotype under *P. ponderosa* subsp. *ponderosa* below.

- *Pinus ponderosa tortuosa* E. -A Carrière, Traité Gén. Conif., Paris, ed. 2, 1867, p. 445, a sport of unknown provenance having twisted branches.

- *Pinus ponderosa* f. *malleti* L. Beissner, Mitt. Deutsch. Dendrol. Ges. 1907, p. 105, a horticultural selection of unknown provenance having reddish bark and long needles.

- *Pinus ponderosa* var. *parryana* (Gordon) W. Robinson, Fl. & Sylva 3, 1905, p. 104, a sport of unknown provenance having numerous, thickly foliated branches, leaves long and drooping, found at Highnam Court near Gloucester, United Kingdom.

- *Pinus ponderosa* var. *sinclairiana* (Gordon) W. Robinson, Fl. & Sylva 3, 1905, p. 104, a sport of unknown provenance having many suberect branches, foliated at tips with short, thick, quite glaucous needles, found at Pampesford Hall near Cambridge, United Kingdom.

A botanical description of the species could be as brief as the original 130 words by P. Lawson and Son (1836) or as long as the five pages written by Sargent (1898). The following description draws heavily from statements and data provided by Lemmon (1888, 1889), Sargent (1898), Haller (1962), Critchfield (1984), Peloquin (1984), and Callaham (2013). This description covers not only unique characteristics of the species but also discloses variability associated with geography for each character. The following description should facilitate identification of ponderosa pine observed in or collected from native stands:

- **Trees** to heights of 80 m (Pacific region).
- **Stem** usually straight and robust; **branches** relatively thick and persistent; usually one whorl per year; usually 3 to 6 in a whorl (2 to 5 in the Rocky Mountains and 1 to 2 in the central High Plains); inserted at a wide to narrow angle from apex of the stem of young trees (average angle, 56° in the

Pacific region, 51° in the Columbia Basin, 48° in the Southwest, 50° in the Rocky Mountains, 36° in the central High Plains).

- **Bark** forms third to fifth year; when tree is mature, with many vertical fissures and furrows and lacking plates, color dark brown, or dark gray, to black; when tree is overmature (older than 150 to 200 years), thick with widely separated and relatively shallow fissures resulting in large plates, color light whitish yellow to yellowish tan in the Pacific region and Columbia Basin, bright cinnamon red in the central High Plains, reddish brown to cinnamon brown in the Southwest; inner abscission layer of individual scales soft and bright yellow or yellowish-tan in color in the Pacific region and the Columbia Basin, reddish-brown to cinnamon in the Southwest, bright cinnamon-red in the central High Plains; tends to be scaly, less fissured, and black or gray in appearance at lower elevations.

- **Xylem oleoresin** odor (discernible in bark crevices warmed by the sun), usually smells like commercial turpentine, in the Pacific region sometimes of lemon rind but never of vanilla or pineapple (characteristic of *P. jeffreyi*), usually abundant presence of the monoterpene *delta* 3-carene (Mirov 1961, Smith 1977).

- **Secondary needles** finely serrate; sharp-tipped; finely lined with stomata on all faces, waxy deposits in stomata appear as lines of small, disconnected, white dots; 144 to 243 mm long and deep yellowish-green in the Pacific region; 130 to 205 mm long and green to blue-green in the Columbia Basin; 92 to 144 mm long and green to blue-green in the Rocky Mountains; 148 to 179 mm long and blue-green in the central High Plains; 112 to 198 mm and green to blue-green in the Southwest; in all regions, paler and shorter at higher elevations and under xeric conditions; generally not glaucous, but becoming glaucous at higher elevations and with the onset of winter; ranging from flexible and in fascicles of three (in the Pacific region, Columbia Basin, and Southwest) to stiff and in fascicles of two or of two and three (in the Rocky Mountains, and High Plains); remaining green on stem an average of 3 to 6 years (ranging 1.4 to 6.5 years in the Pacific region, 2.2 to 7.6 in the Columbia Basin, 2.5 to 5.9 in the Southwest, 3.6 to 7.9 in the Rocky Mountains, 4.1 to 5.0 in the central High Plains), remaining green longer at higher elevations; persisting on branch only a few years, giving a tufted appearance to branches, but extending farther along the branch, giving a fox-tail appearance, at higher elevations in the Rocky Mountains and particularly so in the central High Plains; with two fibrovascular bundles surrounded by a single-celled layer of endodermal cells having thick outer walls; 3 to 7 medial resin ducts external to endoderm; enclosed at the base by sheaths of papery bracts that are, in the first year, 10 to 15 percent of needle length but that weather away to leave a thick, dark brown to black sheath only 4 to 8 mm long on the oldest fascicles.

- **Vegetative shoots** elongating only once each year; in the current year, green or brownish green and viscid in the Pacific region and the Columbia Basin, brown or with white to gray waxy bloom in the Rocky Mountains and the central High Plains, blue or purple waxy bloom or reddish brown in the Southwest.

- **Vegetative buds** covered with ovate acute scales that are conspicuously fringed with fairly short, brownish hairlike projections; scales dark reddish brown (Pacific region) to light chestnut-brown or gray brown; scales closely appressed in most regions but looser in the Pacific region and the Columbia Basin; scales dotted with resin during summer, sometimes covered with resin during winter.

- **Pollen cones** borne in clusters of 5 to 30; long-cylindrical; variable in length and color, 35 to 90 mm and dark reddish brown to reddish purple in the Pacific region, 20 to 70 mm and dark red to reddish purple in the Columbia Basin, 17 to 50 mm and yellow, light pink, or, occasionally, red to purple in the Rocky Mountains, 10 to 25 mm and dark red to reddish purple in the central High Plains.

- **Seed cones** in first year 15 to 25 mm long, on stalks half as long; red on emergence, turning greenish brown to drab gray (in the Pacific region), with short, appressed, mucronate scales, prickles usually erect; when mature, of relatively low density; symmetrical and straight to slightly curved; of medium length (averaging 100 mm in the Pacific region, 89 mm in the Columbia Basin, 75 mm in the Southwest, 71 mm in the Rocky Mountains and the central High Plains), varying in shape from long, ovoid-truncate (in the Pacific region, most but not all of the Columbia Basin, and the Southwest) to ovoid or globoid [Columbia Basin (in the neotype location and elsewhere), Rocky Mountains and central High Plains]; color during second summer variable (apple green to yellow green, but never reddish brown to purple in the Pacific region, polymorphic but typically reddish brown to dark purple, minority of trees having green in the Columbia Basin, green in the Southwest,[16] green to reddish brown to dark purple in

---

[16] Personal communications from Ernest A. Kurmes, Northern Arizona University, Flagstaff, AZ, Ralph A. Read, retired geneticist, USDA Forest Service, and Yan B. Linhart, University of Colorado, Boulder, CO.

the Rocky Mountains[17] and central High Plains, green cones mature to tan and darker pigmented cones mature to reddish or chocolate brown when opening on tree; subsessile and deciduous during the first winter after ripening, very short stalk and a few basal scales usually persisting temporarily on branch after the cone falls.

- **Seed cone scales** relatively few (159 in the Pacific region, 134 to 137 in the Columbia Basin, 112 to 141 in the Rocky Mountains); thin, narrow, slightly concave, and usually rounded at apex; apophysis tawny yellow to fuscous brown, lustrous, only slightly elevated along a transverse keel; umbo salient and forming base of a stout, persistent prickle usually directed outward, but occasionally slightly reflexed; adaxial surface (toward cone axis) slightly concave and dull tawny to red brown; abaxial surface typically dark brown, purplish, or blackish; arranged loosely in two series of spirals, one of 8 rows and the other usually of 5 rows, but occasionally of 13 rows, each row at approximately right angles to the other.

- **Seeds** (body) dark brown or speckled; ovoid acute; rounded in cross section; width about two-thirds of length, averaging 4 to 5 mm; length, 5 to 8 mm (6 to 8 mm in the Pacific region, the Columbia Basin, and the central High Plains, 5 to 7 mm in the Southwest and the Rocky Mountains).

- **Seed wings** thin and semitransparent, pale brown, sometimes darkly streaked with brown; widest at or slightly below midpoint; gradually narrowed to rounded apex; relatively long, that is, 3.3 to 4.3 times length of seed; average length 24.8 mm in the Pacific region, 16.6 mm in the Columbia Basin, 15.5 mm in the Southwest, 16.4 mm in the Rocky Mountains, 16.1 mm in the central High Plains.

The following descriptions emphasize differences among subspecies and do not repeat characteristics they all share in common as ponderosa pine. In the following descriptions, numerical values are means for each subspecies based upon measurements of samples from each of 10 trees at 5 to 50 plot locations and (in parentheses) range between smallest and largest means for plots within each subspecies' geographic area (table 1). Means, standard errors, and ranges for all characteristics were calculated after excluding data from plots in bordering transition zones. In all cases, values for plots within transition zones were intermediate between and overlapping those of adjacent subspecies.

---

[17] Linhart, Y.B. 1998. Personal communication. Professor, University of Colorado, Boulder, CO. Linhart stated that color was always green at low to mid elevations in the Front Range of Colorado; above 2,500 to 3,000 m, some trees have distinctly purple cones.

Table 1—Means (with standard errors (SE) of means, plus range of plot means) derived from multiple measurements on each of 10 trees growing at a varying number of plot locations for *in situ* morphological characteristics of five subspecies of *Pinus ponderosa*

	Subspecies											
	P. ponderosa var. *critchfieldiana*				*P. ponderosa* var. *ponderosa*				*P. ponderosa* var. *scopulorum*			
Characteristic	Mean	1 SE	Range	Plots	Mean	1 SE	Range	Plots	Mean	1 SE	Range	Plots
Foliage:												
Years needles remain green	3.9	0.25	1.4–6.5	30	4.7	0.14	2.2–7.6	50	5.7	0.28	3.6–7.9	23
Foliage length on branch (cm)	25.1	2.4	7.4–52.1	30	26.2	2.2	5.1–84.6	50	21.1	1.7	11.4–42.9	23
Needle color hue	34.8	0.25	32.3–40.4	27	34.3	0.10	31.5–35.2	47	34.3	0.11	32.9–35.0	22
Needle color value	4.4	0.09	3.0–5.0	27	4.4	0.07	3.6–5.1	47	4.5	0.09	3.9–5.4	22
Needle color chroma	4.6	0.08	3.5–5.0	27	4.5	0.06	3.0–5.0	47	4.2	0.14	2.5–5.0	22
Needle length (cm)	19.8	0.44	14.4–24.3	30	16.8	0.29	13.0–20.5	48	11.2	0.27	9.2–14.4	23
Needle length/ fascicle length	8.1	0.28	5.8–12.8	30	7.4	0.15	5.8–10.0	48	6.1	0.22	4.2–7.8	23
Needles per fascicle	3.0	0.002	2.99–3.04	30	3.0	0.002	2.97–3.07	48	2.6	0.06	2.2–3.0	23
Needle thickness (arbitrary units)	45.9	0.49	41.9–54.6	30	47.8	0.51	37.6–58.8	48	46.4	0.68	39.4–53.4	23
Adaxial resin ducts/ needle	0.8	0.04	0.25–1.22	30	0.8	0.04	0.1–1.5	48	0.9	0.10	0.3–2.5	23
Abaxial resin ducts/ needle	2.6	0.15	1.2–3.9	30	2.3	0.13	0.1–4.1	48	2.4	0.15	1.5–3.9	23
Small resin ducts/ needle	3.2	0.19	0.9–4.9	30	2.8	0.17	0.4–5.2	48	3.1	0.25	1.8–6.4	23
Hypodermal cell layers	3.2	0.04	2.7–3.7	30	3.4	0.03	2.7–3.9	48	4.1	0.05	3.6–4.4	23
Branches:												
Branches per whorl	4.4	0.13	2.7–6.0	30	3.7	0.11	1.9–5.6	50	3.0	0.17	2.0–4.6	23
Branch angle (degrees from vertical)	56	1.8	30–75	30	51	1.7	30–79	50	50	2.3	31–76	23
Cone length (mm)	101.4	2.48	63.6–121.7	25	88.7	1.24	72.5–103.0	36	70.7	2.20	52.4–92.6	22
Cone width (mm)	77.1	1.35	56.3–88.6	25	71.6	0.73	63.6–81.4	36	61.5	1.08	53.1–69.1	22
Cone form (width/ length)	0.80	0.03	0.70–1.50	25	0.84	0.03	0.80–1.80	36	0.90	0.02	0.70–1.00	22
Seeds:												
Seed length (mm)	7.5	0.08	6.9–8.1	23	7.6	0.16	6.5–8.4	14	6.3	0.09	5.4–6.9	17
Seed width (mm)	4.9	0.05	4.3–5.3	23	4.9	0.08	4.5–5.5	14	4.1	0.05	3.6–4.6	17
Seed + wing length (mm)	32.3	0.58	24.2–37.0	23	24.8	0.62	20.2–29.5	14	22.9	0.63	18.0–27.6	17
Seed wing widest (base to tip)	0.36	0.02	0.30–0.50	23	0.46	0.01	0.40–0.50	14	0.44	0.02	0.30–0.50	17
Seed form (length/width)	1.52	0.01	1.40–1.60	23	1.57	0.02	1.40–1.70	14	1.52	0.01	1.40–1.60	17
Wing length, absolute (mm)	24.8	0.57	16.1–28.9	23	16.6	0.70	13.0–21.8	14	16.4	0.67	10.0–21.1	17
Wing length, proportional	4.34	0.08	3.00–4.90)	23	3.26	0.10	2.90–4.10)	14	3.62	0.09	3.10–4.30	17

Table 1—Means (with standard errors (SE) of means, plus range of plot means) derived from multiple measurements on each of 10 trees growing at a varying number of plot locations for *in situ* morphological characteristics of five subspecies of *Pinus ponderosa* (continued)

Characteristic	Subspecies							
	P. ponderosa **var.** *brachyptera*				*P. ponderosa* **var.** *readiana*			
	Mean	1 SE	Range	Plots	Mean	1 SE	Range	Plots
Foliage:								
Years needles remain green	4.3	0.18	2.5–5.9	24	4.7	0.18	4.1–5.0	5
Foliage length on branch (cm)	21.8	2.7	6.6–53.8	24	42.2	6.7	25.9–65.0	5
Needle color hue	34.4	0.16	32.8–36.2	24	34.6	0.27	33.5–35.0	5
Needle color value	4.8	0.13	3.7–6.1	24	4.6	0.19	4.1–5.0	5
Needle color chroma	4.0	0.16	2.4–5.0	24	4.8	0.13	4.3–5.0	5
Needle length (cm)	114.7	0.45	11.2–19.8	24	15.6	0.57	14.8–17.9	5
Needle length/ fascicle length	6.4	0.26	4.5–9.9	23	9.3	0.36	8.2–10.4	5
Needles per fascicle	3.0	0.03	2.7–3.5	24	2.4	0.11	2.2–2.8	5
Needle thickness (arbitrary units)	44.8	0.87	34.4–51.1	24	49.7	0.61	47.4–51.0	5
Adaxial resin ducts/ needle	1.2	0.09	0.7–2.4	24	1.5	0.35	0.6–2.6	5
Abaxial resin ducts/ needle	2.4	0.18	0.8–4.4	24	3.9	0.60	2.1–5.6	5
Small resin ducts/ needle	3.4	0.27	1.1–6.4	24	5.4	0.98	2.5–8.2	5
Hypodermal cell layers	4.1	0.06	3.4–4.5	24	4.7	0.06	4.5–4.9	5
Branches:								
Branches per whorl	3.4	0.25	1.6–6.6	23	1.3	0.11	1.1–1.6	5
Branch angle (degrees from vertical)	3.1		30–79	24	36	1.9	31–40	5
Cone length (mm)	74.9	2.51	60.2–99.2	20	71.1	2.46	64.8–77.1	5
Cone width (mm)	62.6	1.77	47.6–75.6	20	63.3	2.18	58.6–68.9	5
Cone form (width/ length)	0.86	0.02	0.80–1.00	20	0.90	0.03	0.80–1.00	5
Seeds:								
Seed length (mm)	6.4	0.18	5.1–7.4	16	7.0	0.12	6.5–7.2	5
Seed width (mm)	4.3	0.09	3.8–4.9	16	4.5	0.10	4.2–4.7	5
Seed + wing length (mm)	23.3	0.68	18.2–26.2	15	23.1	0.78	20.8–24.9	5
Seed wing widest (base to tip)	0.44	0.01,	0.40–0.50	15	0.48	0.02,	0.40–0.50	5
Seed form (length/width)	1.48	0.02,	1.30–1.60	16	1.56	0.02,	1.50–1.60	5
Wing length, absolute (mm)	15.5	1.47,	15.1–19.3	16	16.1	0.68,	14.3–17.7	5
Wing length, proportional	3.59	0.07,	3.30–4.00	15	3.30	0.06,	3.20–3.50	5

Five Subspecies

1. *Pinus ponderosa* Douglas ex C. Lawson subsp. *ponderosa*, Columbia ponderosa pine—

Type: The name, as used by C. Lawson, was linked to "small plants in pots... (and) a specimen (eight years old), perhaps the finest in Scotland, growing in the Caledonian Horticultural Society's Gardens, Inverleith Row. ... Introduced by Mr. Douglas from the west coast of North America in 1828" (protologue); [holotype: not found; a specimen with one fascicle of needles marked "ex K in MO," according to Lauria:[18]

> ...was donated to G. Engelmann on the occasion of his visit to Europe in 1869 and originates from a specimen which, as far as we know today, did not serve as holotype to the author of the protologue of the first description of *Pinus ponderosa*. Therefore, this single fascicle does not represent type material.

[According to Lauria and the journal of Douglas (1836), specimens (but not a type specimen) were collected, 11–12 May 1826, near Spokane (Spokane County), Washington. According to Lauria, seeds collected that fall, probably by John Work, perhaps in the vicinity of Kettle Falls (Stevens County) or the Pend Oreille River (Pend Oreille County), Washington, presumably were given in April 1827 to Douglas who returned with them to London. Evidence presented by Lauria leaves no doubt as to either proper application of name or nonexistence of a type.]

Absent a type, a neotype is designated here: Washington, Stevens County, Farm to Market Road Kelly to Highway 395, at Alex Lewis Place, Barstow Bridge, South to Napoleon Railroad Siding, Colville National Forest, about 10 ms south of Orient, bench of Kettle River, sandy loam soil, southwest-facing slope, pure ponderosa pine stand, approximate latitude 48°46' N, longitude 118°07' W, 1,300 to 1,500 ft, T37-38N, R37E, Sec. 33, 4, 16, WM; 16 Sep 1955, *Hugh Cheyney & F.W. Cony, s. n. IFG plot 118* (neotype: UC; isoneotypes: A, IFG, K, NA, NEB). Well's (1964) progeny number MSFG 2102 was from the neotype.

- *Pinus ponderosa* f. *crispata* F.G. von Schwerin, Mitt. Deutsch. Dendrol. Ges. 1919, 325. A sport having sickle-shaped needles. From an unknown provenance near Kamloops, British Columbia. Placed in synonymy here on basis of geography.

---

[18] Personal communication from Friedrich Lauria, Naturhistorische Museum Wien, Vienna, Austria, February 5, 1992.

- *Pinus washoensis* H. Mason & Stockw., Madroño 8: 61, 1945.—*Pinus ponderosa* var. *washoensis* (H. Mason & Stockw.) Ting W.S., Univ. Calif. Publ. Geol. Sci. 58:116. 1966 —*Pinus ponderosa* subsp. *washoensis* (H. Mason & Stockw.) E. Murray, Kalmia 12:23. 1982.—Type: Nevada, Washoe County, Mount Rose; 3 mi east of highway summit, south side of Galena Creek; elev. 8,100 ft.; 4 August 1940, *H.L. Mason, 12,370* (UC, 692993).

This particular neotype for *Pinus ponderosa* was chosen for three reasons. First, it is typical of the ponderosa pine that would have been available to Work, the Hudson Bay trader who is believed to have collected the seed that Douglas imported to England. Second, it was collected only 12 mi (19 km) north-northwest of Work's headquarters at Kettle Falls, Washington, where Douglas is presumed to have received the seeds in April 1827 on his overland return to Hudson Bay. Third, it was part (trees in plots 118 and 318) of range-wide collections in 1955 and 1956 of ponderosa pine (Callaham 2013) (fig. 2).

The common name, Columbia ponderosa pine, is chosen because most of the range of this subspecies is within the watershed of the Columbia River and its tributaries. Outside of this watershed, it occurs only in the Fraser River watershed in British Columbia, and in southern Oregon. Weidman (1939) called this subspecies "north plateau race," probably because the geologic area sometimes is called the Columbia Plateau. Application of the word "plateau" is deemed inappropriate because the geographic area is everything but an elevated, level, tableland. The term "Inland Empire," applied to the area surrounding Spokane, Washington, also was rejected because it applies only to a fraction of the range of this subspecies.

Columbia ponderosa pine is characterized by three needles per fascicle (2.97 to 3.07). Needles from the middle of the annual growth are long, 168 (130 to 205) mm. They also are thickest, except for needles of subsp. *readiana*. Needles have the fewest small resin ducts: 0.8 adaxial resin ducts (0.1 to 1.5) plus 2.3 abaxial resin ducts (0.1 to 4.1). Hypodermal cell layers in needle corners average 3.4 (2.7 to 3.9). Needles remain green an average of 4.7 years (2.2 to 7.6).

Trees display an intermediate number of branches per whorl, 3.7 (1.9 to 5.6). Branch angle from vertical in tree tops is relatively flat, 51 (30 to 79) degrees, and like that of most other subspecies except *readiana*.

Color of immature cones during second growing season is dark red to purple on the majority of trees but green on occasional trees (Smith 1981). Mature cones (fig. 3) usually are intermediate in both length, 88.7 mm (72.5 to 103), and width, 71.6 mm (63.6 to 81.4). The result is a cone of relatively elongate form factor, 0.84 (0.80 to 1.80).

Figure 3—One selected cone from each of six trees, neotype of *Pinus ponderosa* subsp. *ponderosa*.

Seed body is longest for the species, 7.6 mm (6.5 to 8.4). Along with those of subsp. *critchfieldiana*, seeds are widest for the species, 4.9 mm (4.5 to 5.5). Seeds are longest in relation to width for the species, form factor 1.57 (1.40 to 1.70). Length of seed body plus wing, 24.8 mm (20.2 to 29.5), resembles that of most inland subspecies but is much shorter than in Pacific ponderosa pine subsp. *critchfieldiana*. Length of seed wing alone, 16.6 mm (13.0 to 21.8), also resembles that of other inland subspecies but is substantially less than in subsp. *critchfieldiana*. Proportional length of seed wing, as a multiple of seed (body) length, 3.26 (2.90 to 4.10), is lowest for the species.

Vegetative shoots, before lignification, are green and viscid.[19] Buds are reddish brown to chestnut brown with loosely appressed scales (Wright et al. 1969).

Monoterpenes in xylem oleoresin of Columbia ponderosa pines are characterized by very high *delta*-3-carene (48 to 53 percent), less myrcene (19 to 21 percent),

---

[19] Personal communication from Gerald Rehfeldt, geneticist, USDA Forest Service, Intermountain Research Station, Moscow, ID.

and little to very little limonene (7 to 12 percent); resin exuding from xylem is colorless to light amber in color (Smith 1977).

Cone Dimorphism

Trees at the location from which the neotype was selected were typical Columbia ponderosa pine except for one notable trait—a high proportion of trees produced dimorphic cones (fig. 4). Two of four mature, seed-bearing cones collected in 1994 from a single tree were globose (55 mm wide by 55 mm long, form [width divided by length] 1.00), another cone was ovoid (58 mm wide by 64 mm long, form 0.91). The fourth cone was elongated (73 mm wide by 87 mm long; form, 0.84). Range in length of one long and six short cones from a second tree (in 1994) was 57 to 83 mm (mean 64.3 mm), and range in form was 0.77 to 0.90 (mean 0.84). But all seven cones from a third tree (in 1994) were short, 52 to 65 mm (mean 59.0 mm); their form ranged from 0.74 to 0.96 (mean 0.85).

This finding, in 1994, that a tree produced only short cones, caused me to reexamine my basic data for the neotype. These data were collected in 1955 from five cones from each of 10 (or fewer) trees (Callaham 2013, plot 118). I ascertained that one of the 10 trees sampled in 1955 produced only short (67 to 77 mm, ovoid–globose) cones; seven of those trees produced only longer (88 to 111 mm, elongate–ovoid) cones; two of those trees produced both short (70 to 73 mm) cones and long (97 to 98 mm) cones identical to two of the three trees sampled in 1994. Such an allometric shift as this can be under simple genetic control (Gottlieb 1984).

When I first observed dimorphism in cones collected in 1994 from the location of the neotype, I thought dimorphic cones were extremely unusual for ponderosa pine. That observation led me to reexamine my basic data on cone length for Columbia and Pacific ponderosa pines (Callaham 2013). Masked by my original calculations of mean cone-length per plot were differences among trees in both cone length and cone form that were highly significant statistically. (A negative correlation exists between these characters; shorter cones are proportionally wider; as cone length decreases cone form increases.) Pronounced cone dimorphism (one to several cones 35 to 60 percent longer than the shorter cones) occurred on 16 of approximately 570 trees (= 2.6 percent) on 12 of 59 plots (= 20 percent), 1 of 10 trees on nine plots, 2 of 10 trees on two plots, and 3 of 10 trees on one plot. Pronounced cone dimorphism was an infrequent but not unusual phenomenon in the two western subspecies of ponderosa pine.

Figure 4—Cone dimorphism is apparent on two of three pairs of largest and smallest cones from each of three trees, neotype of *Pinus ponderosa* subsp. *ponderosa.*

Besides the neotype—from a tree located in northeastern Washington—trees bearing dimorphic cones were located along the Kootenay River, north of Kimberly, British Columbia (plot 97), at two locations in northern Idaho (plots 106 and 120), at two locations along the border between Idaho and Montana (plots 109, 182, and 183), at two locations in central Oregon (plots 31 and 41), and at three locations in the northern Coast Range in California (plots 49, 88, and 195). Dimorphic cones also were found on 10 of 17 plots of southwestern ponderosa pine.

Cones shorter than 79 mm and ovoid/globose in shape were collected from 1 to 9 of 10 trees on most of my 37 plots within the range of Columbia ponderosa pine. I was surprised to find that such cones were collected from 1 or 2 of 10 trees (in four plots from 3 to 6 of 10 trees) on two-thirds of my 22 plots in the range of Pacific ponderosa pine. My conclusions were:

- Individual trees of Columbia ponderosa pines frequently bear small, ovoid/globose cones that are indistinguishable from cones of Washoe pine.
- Trees of Pacific ponderosa pine bear Washoe-like cones less frequently.

Pinus washoensis versus Columbia ponderosa pine—

Lauria,[20] after studying trees in the United Kingdom, concluded that "all cones seen from trees documented to originate from Douglas' introduction are decidedly Washoe-like, that means medium to small, dense, egg-shaped/globose and not of relatively elongate form ... ." His finding suggests that Douglas' seed was collected from one or more trees (similar to trees 2, 9, 10, and 13 on plot 118) that bore only smaller, ovoid–globose cones typically associated with Washoe pine.

My shorter, ovoid–globose cones (figs. 3 and 4) are indistinguishable from cones of Washoe pine. Upon reexamining my data from 45 cones collected in 1955 from nine trees near the type location of that taxon (plot 200 = Wells' 2292), I found that cones ranged in length from 48 to 82 mm, and ranged in form from 0.61 to 1.16. Most cones were ovoid to globose, form 0.8 to 1.0. Obviously, the many Columbia ponderosa pines that produced smaller cones were indistinguishable from *Pinus washoensis*.

This finding caused me to reexamine the type specimen of *Pinus washoensis*; whereon, I noted an annotation by T.C. Brayshaw, 5 Feb. 1986: "This material does not exceed the limits of variability, in any character visible, of *Pinus ponderosa* Dougl. ex Laws. var. *ponderosa*, North Plateau (Columbia) race, as found in British Columbia."

---

[20] See footnote 2.

Remembering admonitions and numerous comments from Lauria,[21] I reviewed evidences and discussions presented by Haller (1961, 1965a), Critchfield and Allenbaugh (1965), Critchfield and Little (1966), Little (1979), Critchfield (1984), Ting (1966), Niebling and Conkle (1990), Smith (1967, 1971, 1977, 1981), Wells (1964), and Rehfeldt (1999). Wells (1964a) wrote about Washoe pine: "It was very different from all other progenies (of the Pacific ecotype)." Notably, he failed to compare it to Columbia ponderosa pine. Haller (1965a) was first to propose that Washoe pine be included in the North Plateau race of ponderosa pine. After reexamining my data [my plot 200's 10 trees (= Wells' 2292) vs. 37 plots (= 370 trees) of Columbia ponderosa pine], I concluded Washoe pine and Columbia ponderosa pine do not differ significantly in:

- *In situ* characteristics of size, shape, or immature color of cones, length and width of seeds, length of seed wing, or length, width, and anatomy of needles
- Monoterpenes in xylem resin
- Many characteristics of seedlings in the nursery.

Using Wells' data, Critchfield (1984) concluded "Washoe pine was more like the North Plateau (Columbia) race..." After examining Wells' data I concluded there were many similarities and only sporadic significant differences between Washoe pine and Columbia ponderosa pine.[22] Washoe pine (one plot versus seven plots) differed significantly in:

- Length of secondary needles (shorter than four plots)
- Susceptibility to winter injury (less than four plots)
- Trees forming terminal buds at age 1 (fewer than five plots)
- Bud scale exsertion (more than five plots)
- Date growth started (later than seven plots)
- Heights at ages 1 or 2 (less than six or seven plots).

All of these significant differences could simply reflect inherent adaptations of Washoe pine to grow at a very high elevation (2554 m, 8,300 ft.) and survive in the deep, late-melting snowpack of the Sierra Nevada. All of the foregoing evidences led me to conclude that Washoe pine and Columbia ponderosa pine are taxonomically synonymous.

---

[21] Lauria, F. 1991, 1992, 1994, 1995. Personal communications. Naturhistorische Museum Wien, Vienna, Austria.

[22] Washoe pine [my plot 200 (elev. 2554 m) = Wells' 2292] versus Columbia ponderosa pine [my plots 34 (elev. 680 m), 40 (elev. 1540 m), 53 (elev. 1850 m), 100 (elev. 520 m), 102 (elev. 550 m), 118 (elev. 430 m), 123 (elev. 1290 m) = respectively Wells' 2032, 2034, 2045, 2124, 2134, 2102, 2205].

2. *Pinus ponderosa* Douglas ex C. Lawson subsp. *critchfieldiana* Callaham subsp. *nov.*, Pacific ponderosa pine—

Type: California, Placer County, Forest Hill, northern edge of flat ridge top, about 50 ft west of northern edge of Forest Hill Ranger Station, Tahoe National Forest, approximate latitude 39°01'N, longitude 120°49'W, 3,200 ft, T14N, R10E, Sec. 35, MDM, 25 Sep. 1955, *Glen E. Sindel s. n. IFG plot 68* (holotype: UC; isotypes: A, IFG, K, NA, NEB). Well's (1964) progeny number MSFG 2056 was from the type.

- *Pinus benthamiana* Hartweg, J. Hort. Soc. London 2:189. 1847.—*Pinus ponderosa* var. *benthamiana* (Hartweg) Vasey, Cat. For. Trees, U.S. Govt. Print. Office. 30. 1876.—*P. ponderosa* var. *benthamiana* (Hartweg) Lemmon (1888), comb. superfl.—Type: California, Santa Cruz Co., vicinity of Santa Cruz (actually Bonny Doon), 24 Aug 1846, *Hartweg s.n.* [holotype: not found; John Strother found a specimen in MO, 899036, labeled "*P. Benthamian* (*sic*) California 1847" that appears to be type material. Description and type locality leave no doubt as to application of name.]

- *Pinus beardsleyi* A. Murray, Edinb. New Phil. J. Ser. 2. 1:286, pl. 6. 1855.—*Pinus ponderosa* var. *beardsleyi* (A. Murray) A. Kellogg, Forest Trees Calif., Sacramento, Calif., 44.1882—Type: holotype: not found; specimen labeled "*Pinus bairdsleyi*" by Engelmann, 13 Sept 1869, is in MO;[23] text, figure, and Engelmann's specimen leave no doubt as to application of this name.

- *Pinus craigana* A. Murray, Edinb. New Phil. J. Ser. 2. 1:288, pl. 7. 1855.—Type: holotype: not found; a specimen, perhaps the holotype, labeled "*ponderosa*" by Engelmann, 30 Aug 1869 is in MO, 3574205;[24] text, figure, and Engelmann's labeled specimen leave no doubt as to application of this name.

- *Pinus ponderosa* var. *nigricans* Lemmon, Bull. Calif. State Board For. 7:8. 1889—Type: holotype: not found; text leaves no doubt as to application of this name.

- *Pinus ponderosa* var. *pacifica* Haller, Aliso 29(1): 53–57.—Type: in herbarium UCSB, J.R. Haller 10205 (holotype UCSB 69943), leaves no doubt as to application of this name.

---

[23] Xerographed copy of specimen provided by Friedrich Lauria, Naturhistorische Museum Wien, Vienna, Austria, February 28, 1994.

[24] See footnote 2.

Latin description—*Differt a P. ponderosa* subsp. *ponderosa ramis* 4.4 (2.7–6.0) [vs. 3.7 (1.9 to 5.6)] *per verticillum, foliis* 198 (144 to 243) mm *longis* [vs. 168 (130 to 205)] mm *longis, seminum alis* 4.34 plo (3.00 to 4.90) [vs. 3.26 plo (2.90 to 4.10)] *seminibus longioribus, strobilis maturescentibus viridis vel luteo-viridis* [vs. *plerumque rubris vel purpureis sed aliquando viridis*]. *Differt a P. ponderosa* subsp. *brachyptera viridis foliis retentis* 3.9 (1.4 to 6.5) *annis* [vs. 4.7 (2.2 to 7.6) *annis*], *foliifer segmentis ramorum* 251 (74 to 521) mm *longis* [vs. 262 (51 to 846) mm *longis*], *angulis ramorum* 56 (30 to 75) *gradis* [vs. 51 (30 to 79) *gradis*], *foliis* 198 (144 to 243) mm *longis* [vs. 168 (130 to 205) mm *longis*], *canalibus resiniferis adaxialibus* 0.8 (0.2–1.2) [vs. 0.8 (0.1–1.5)] *per folium*, et *stratis cellularum hypodermatum* in *angulis foliorum* in *sectione transversali* 3.2 (2.7 to 3.7) [vs. 3.4 (2.7 to 3.9)].

The subspecific name honors Dr. William Burke Critchfield (1923–1989), my ever-helpful colleague during 42 years. Together we completed our undergraduate degrees in forestry and doctorates in botany at the University of California at Berkeley. Then he served with distinction as botanist at Maria Moors Cabot Foundation, Harvard University (1956–1958). He replaced me (1958) as geneticist at the IFG at Placerville, California, and continued there until his retirement in 1988. As one of only seven Pioneering Research Scientists in the USDA Forest Service, his work spanned plant growth and morphology, plant geography, pine hybridization and evolution, and paleobotany. His name is respected around the world for his many contributions that clarified taxonomy, geographic distribution, and genetic relationships among pines. He substantially added to our understanding of ponderosa pine and of this particular subspecies. In his time, no one knew more about pines of the world than he.

Pacific ponderosa pine is chosen as a common name because this subspecies grows in three states—California, Oregon, and Washington, all fronting on the Pacific Ocean. "Coastal ponderosa pine" (Haller 1965) is not chosen because the subspecies grows primarily in interior valleys and mountain ranges. Only rarely does it grow in sight of the Pacific Ocean.

Pacific ponderosa pine has these characteristics that distinguish it from other subspecies:

- Briefest retention of green needles, 3.9 years (1.4 to 6.5)
- Most branches per whorl, 4.4 (2.7 to 6.0)
- Greatest branch angle from vertical, 56 (30 to 75) degrees
- Longest needles, 198 (144 to 243) mm
- Most uniform display of three needles per fascicle (range 2.99 to 3.04)
- Fewest adaxial resin ducts in needles, 0.8 (0.2 to 1.2)
- Fewest layers of hypodermal cells in needle corners, 3.2 (2.7 to 3.7)

- Longest cones, 101 (64 to 122) mm (fig. 5)
- Widest cones, 77 (56 to 89) mm
- Cones with lowest form factor, 0.80 (0.70 to 1.50)
- Longest seeds, 7.45 (6.9 to 8.1) mm
- Widest seeds (but only very slightly wider than those of subsp. *ponderosa*)
- Longest seed plus seed wing, 32.3 (24 to 37) mm
- Longest seed wing, 24.8 (16.1 to 28.9) mm
- Greatest proportional length of the seed wing, 4.3 times seed length (3.0 to 4.9)
- Seed cones during second summer green to yellow green in color (Smith 1981)

Figure 5—One selected cone from each of five trees, type of *Pinus ponderosa* subsp. *critchfieldiana.*

- Pollen cones longest for species, 40 to 90 mm (dried), ranging in color from dark red to red purple (Critchfield 1984)
- Highest proportion of *beta*-pinene in xylem oleoresin (Smith 1977).

Pacific ponderosa pine differs significantly from Columbia ponderosa pine (table 1) by having:

- More branches per whorl
- 18 percent longer needles
- 50 percent longer seed wing
- Greater proportional length of seed wing
- Maturing seed cones green to yellow green vs. usually red to purple (occasionally green) during the second summer.

Pacific ponderosa pine differs markedly from Rocky Mountains ponderosa pine (table 1) by having:

- Needles retained almost 2 years less
- At least one more branch per whorl and wider branching angle
- Needles that are 75 percent longer but slightly thinner
- No occurrence of two needles per fascicle (confirmed by Read 1980)
- Cones 42 percent longer and tend to be more elongate in form
- Seeds (body) longer by 1 mm, and wider (confirmed by Read 1980)
- Seed wings half again as long
- Seedlings failed to form secondary needles during first year of growth (Wells 1964), seedlings of Rocky Mountains ponderosa pine rarely did so
- Foliage color on first-year seedlings during August yellow green to green, Rocky Mountains ponderosa pine green to blue- green (Wells 1964)
- Buds reddish brown to chestnut brown with loosely appressed scales (Wright et al. 1969).

Pacific ponderosa pine differs significantly from southwestern ponderosa pine (table 1) by having:

- Green needles retained almost a half-year less
- Longer needle-bearing segments of branches
- Wider branch angle
- Needles one-third longer
- Only two-thirds as many adaxial resin ducts per needle
- Fewer layers of hypodermal layers in needle corners
- Longer seed body (confirmed by Read 1980) and much longer seed wings
- Seedlings with significantly more cotyledons, attributed to larger seeds by Read (1980)

- Fewer secondary needles
- Hardly any seedlings form secondary needles during the first year of growth (Wells 1964) , but 45 to 100 percent (depending on seed source) of southwestern seedlings formed secondary needles
- Foliage color on first-year seedlings during August yellow green to green while that of southwestern ponderosa pine was green to blue green
- Stem color during second year of growth green to light green while southwestern ponderosa pine varied from light green to gray (Wells 1964) because of a waxy bloom (Read 1980)
- Current vegetative shoots usually green to brown and viscid or resinous to touch, southwestern ponderosa pine shoots usually covered by purplish waxy bloom (Read 1980
- Monoterpenes predominantly *delta*-3-carene (37 to 55 percent) vs. 15 to 42 percent in southwestern ponderosa pine (Smith 1977)
- Very low amount of *alpha*-pinene (12 to 29 percent) vs. 38 to 50 percent in southwestern ponderosa pine (Smith 1977)
- Oleoresin yellow to dark amber vs. colorless to light amber exuding from southwestern ponderosa pine (Smith 1977).

Pacific ponderosa pine differs significantly from central high plains ponderosa pine (table 1) by having:

- Only 60 percent of green foliage length on branches
- Four times as many branches per whorl
- Branch angle tending closer to horizontal
- Needles 30 percent longer; more needles per fascicle
- About half as many adaxial needle resin ducts
- Two-thirds as many abaxial needle resin ducts
- Two-thirds as many hypodermal cell layers
- Cones 45 percent longer and 22 percent wider
- Cone form less ovate
- Seed plus wing length 40 percent longer
- Seed wings 50 percent longer
- Hardly any seedlings formed secondary needles during the first year of growth vs. 36 to 76 percent (depending on seed source) formed secondary needles (Wells 1964), confirmed by Read (1980)

- Summer foliage color on first-year seedlings (grown in Michigan) yellow-green to green vs. blue-green (Wells 1964)

- Winter foliage color, when grown in the Great Plains, green vs. purple (Read 1980)

- Oleoresin monoterpenes characterized by high amounts of both *beta*-pinene (27 to 45 percent) and *delta*-3-carene (35 to 41 percent) plus considerable myrcene (20 to 21 percent) and limonene (18 to 22 percent) vs. central high plains, not studied by Smith (1977).

3. *Pinus ponderosa* Douglas ex C. Lawson subsp. *scopulorum* (Engelm. in S. Watson) E. Murray, Kalmia 12:23. (July) 1982, Rocky Mountains (not Mountain) ponderosa pine—

Pinus ponderosa var. *scopulorum* Engelm. in S. Watson, Bot. California 2:126. 1879 [1880][25]—*Pinus ponderosa scopulorum* (Engelm. in S. Watson) Sudworth, U.S. Department of Agriculture Division of Forestry, Bulletin 14: 20. 1897.—*Pinus scopulorum* (Engelm. in S. Watson) Lemmon, Garden and Forest 10:183. 1897.—*Pinus ponderosa* subsp. *scopulorum* (Engelm. in S. Watson) W. A. Weber, Phytologia 51: 374. (August) 1982, *comb. superfl.*

Type: No specimens or locations cited in protologue; referred to in protologue only as "*P. ponderosa* of the Rocky Mountain floras."—Lauria[26] provided a list of 19 specimens of *Pinus ponderosa* var. *scopulorum* in MO that he attests were "studied by Dr. George Engelmann for the publication of the 'Abietineae' (1879) in 'Botany of California, 1880'." A search by John Strother (University of California Herbarium at Berkeley) through holdings of *Pinus ponderosa* at the MO herbarium, where most of Engelmann's specimens were deposited, failed to reveal any specimens that were designated or could be construed as type of *P. ponderosa* var. *scopulorum*.

To fix application of name *scopulorum*, a neotype is designated here: *Pinus ponderosa* Douglas ex P. Lawson & Lawson subsp. *scopulorum* (Engelm.) E. Murray, Kalmia 12:23. (July) 1982, Rocky Mountains ponderosa pine—

---

[25] See footnote 2.

[26] Same source as footnote 2, personal communication, February 5, 1992.

Neotype: Colorado, El Paso Co., granitic ridge; steep, south-facing 30 to 40 degree slope; young, all-aged stand, about 6.5 mi south of Woodland Park Post Office, on Railroad Road; up Log Creek to Rampart Range Road, then south to the cattle guard; plot sign S. 35° W., 25 links, from SW corner of the concrete on the cattle guard; approximate latitude 39°00'N, long. 105°00'W, 9, 100 ft, fall (probably late September) 1955, (*W.M. Johnson*), *s. n. IFG plot 21* (neotype: UC; isotypes: A, IFG, K, NA, NEB). Well's (1964) progeny number MSFG 2164 was from the neotype. Read's (1980) collection designated as origin 763 was from vicinity of the neotype.

- *Pinus ponderosa pendula* H. Sargent, Gard. Chron. 10 (n.s.): 236, f. 42. 1878, not *Pinus pendula* Aiton, 1789, a sport having weeping branches from an unknown provenance of *P. ponderosa fide* Sudworth (1897).—*Pinus ponderosa penduliformis* Sudworth, Bull. U.S.D.A. Div. For. 14: 21. 1897, *nom. superfl., illegit.*—*Pinus ponderosa* f. *pendula* (H. Sargent) R. A. Vines, Trees, Shrubs ... Southwest, Austin, TX. 1960, 19.

- *Pinus ponderosa* f. *nana* L. Beissner, Mitt. Deutsch. Dendrol. Ges. 1912, 365, a sport having a dwarf habit found near Coal Creek, Jefferson Co., Colorado by F. von Holdt. Type: unknown; name placed in synonymy here on basis of geography.

- *Pinus ponderosa* f. *koolhaas* J. L. Mol, Jaarb Ned. Dendrol. Ver. (1952-) 1953, 74, a sport of dwarf habit having contorted weeping branches. Type: unknown; name placed in synonymy here on basis of geography.

Conkle and Critchfield (1988) wrote: "The compact, brushlike, bushy-tuft (scopulate) appearance of ponderosa foliage in the Rocky Mountains differed from the open, plume-like foliage in western areas, and var. *scopulorum* was coined in recognition of that characteristic ... ."

Obviously they were referring to the Latin adjectives *scopulatus* or *scoparius*, meaning like a broom or brush. However, Engelmann's protologue, "of the Rocky Mountain flora," refers to the genitive plural of the Latin noun *scopulus* (meaning of the rock, ledge, shelf, or cliff) and, indirectly, to the Rocky Mountains, often shortened to Rockies.

Readers should note my purposeful choice of a new common name, Rocky Mountains ponderosa pine. This subspecies grows in the Rocky Mountains, not on Rocky Mountain. Would one call the trees growing in the Black Hills, Black Hill ponderosa pine? Of course not. So I contend that Rocky Mountains ponderosa pine, being the correct common name, should be used henceforth.

Rocky Mountains ponderosa pine has many distinctive, statistically significant characteristics: means (ranges):

- Years needles stay green, 5.7 (3.6 to 7.9)
- Branches per whorl, 3.0 (2.0 to 4.6)
- Branching angle, 50 (31 to 76) degrees
- Needle length, 112 (92 to 144) mm
- Needles per fascicle, 2.6 (2.2 to 3.0)
- Hypodermal cell layers, 4.1 (3.6 to 4.4)
- Cone length, 70.7 (52 to 93) mm (fig. 6)
- Cone form factor, 0.90 (0.70 to 1.00)
- Seed (body) length, 6.3 (5.4 to 6.9) mm
- Seed width, 4.1 (3.6 to 4.6) mm
- Seed form, 1.52 (1.4 to 1.6)
- Seed plus wing length, 22.9 (18 to 28) mm
- Seed wing's absolute length, 16.4 (10 to 21) mm
- Pollen cones yellow, often light pink, occasionally dark red.[27]

Figure 6—One selected cone from each of seven trees, neotype of *Pinus ponderosa* subsp. *scopulorum*.

---

[27] Read, R.A. 1992. Personal communication: "Pollen cones are both yellow and reddish, varying tree-to-tree, probably in equal quantities."

Rocky Mountains ponderosa pine contrasts with Columbia ponderosa pine (table 1) by having:

- Needles only two-thirds as long and stiffened by more hypodermal cell layers
- More frequently two rather than three needles per fascicle (confirmed by Read 1980)
- Cones ovoid rather than elongate form
- Cone color always green at low to mid elevations, at high elevations (above 2500 m) sometimes distinctly purple[28] as in Columbia ponderosa pine
- Seed plus wing length shorter
- Absolute length of seed wing shorter
- Seeds less elongate and smaller (Read 1980)
- Cotyledons fewer
- Shoots displaying more waxy bloom
- Needles more appressed to stem
- Pollen cones usually yellow (Critchfield 1984), but in Columbia basin dark red to red purple (Critchfield 1984)
- Pollen cone color yellow, often light pink, occasionally dark pink to purple (Linhart).[29]

Read (1980), comparing his many seed sources of Rocky Mountains ponderosa pine to only one seed source of Pacific ponderosa pine, observed:

- Seeds were small versus large
- Germination was quick versus slow
- Cotyledons were few versus many (which he attributed to differences in seed size)
- Winter foliage color on seedlings was purple versus green
- Secondary needles were many versus few
- Needles were appressed versus divergent
- Buds were grayish brown with closely appressed scales (Wright et al. 1969).

Proportions of monoterpenes in xylem oleoresin distinguish Rocky Mountains ponderosa pine from other subspecies (Smith 1977). Northern Rocky Mountains ponderosa pine growing in central Montana, Wyoming, and South Dakota differs significantly from Columbia ponderosa pine growing to the west (more *alpha*-pinene, more *beta*-pinene, less *delta*-3-carene, and less myrcene). Western Rocky Mountains ponderosa pine growing in Utah and Nevada differs significantly from Columbia ponderosa pine growing to the north (more *alpha*-pinene, less *delta*-3-

---

[28] Linhart, Y.B. 1998. Professor, University of Colorado, Boulder, CO.
[29] See footnote 2.

carene, and less myrcene). Rocky Mountains ponderosa pine differs from Pacific ponderosa pine by having less *beta*-pinene, more *delta*-3-carene, less myrcene, and less limonene. It differs from southwestern ponderosa pine by having less *alpha*-pinene, more *beta*-pinene, more *delta*-3-carene, and more myrcene.

4. *Pinus ponderosa* Douglas ex C. Lawson subsp. *readiana* Callaham, subsp. *nov.*, central high plains ponderosa pine—

Type: Nebraska, Keya Paha Co., south aspect of canyons and breaks sloping from tableland to Niobrara River valley, ca. 1.7 mi northwest of Niobrara River bridge at Carnes P.O., 11 mi. north, 1 mi east of Bassett, approx. lat. 42°45'N, long. 99°32'W, 2,100 ft, 5 Oct. 1955, *R. A. Read s. n. IFG plot 23* (holotype: UC; isotypes: A, IFG, K, NA, NEB). Well's (1964) progeny number MSFG 2180 was from the type.

Latin description—*Differt* a *P. ponderosa* subsp. *scopulorum ramis* 1.3 (1.1to 1.6) [vs. 3.0 (2.0 to 4.6) *per verticillum, foliiferis segmentis ramorum* 422 (259 to 650) mm *longis* [vs. 211 (114 to 429) mm], *foliis* 156 (148 to 179) mm *longis* [vs. 112 (92 to 144) mm], *canalibus resiniferis abaxialibus* 3.9 (2.1 to 5.6) [vs. 2.4 (1.5 to 3.9) *per folium, canalibus resiniferis adaxialibus* 1.5 (0.6–2.6) [vs. 0.9 (0.3 to 2.5)] *per folium*, and *seminum alis* 16.1 (14.3–17.7) mm *longis* [vs. 16.4 (10.0–21.1) mm].

The subspecific name honors Ralph A. Read (1916–2001) who served with distinction until his retirement in 1979 as a research forester and geneticist at the USDA Forest Service's Shelterbelt (now Agroforestry) Laboratory in Lincoln, Nebraska. His postgraduate studies were at Yale University, School of Forestry (MF, 1949) and at the University of Nebraska in botany and genetics (1960–1961). His definitive research substantially added to our understanding of patterns of inherent variation in ponderosa pines growing in the High Plains and the Rocky Mountains. He was the authority on the variability and ecology of ponderosa pine growing east of the Continental Divide.

The common name recognizes occurrence of *P. ponderosa* subsp. *readiana* in the central High Plains but not in either the northern or southern high plains, where subsp. *scopulorum* prevails.

The sparse, upright branching habit of this subspecies is unique. It has fewest branches per whorl of any subspecies, 1.3 (1.1 to 1.6), and narrowest branching angle, 36 (31 to 40) degrees. Green needles extend much farther along the branch than in any other subspecies, 422 mm (259 to 650), making branches look like the long tail of a fox. Needles are widest for the species and have thickest layers of hypodermal cells, 4.7 (4.5 to 4.9), making them very stiff. Needles have greatest number of small resin ducts—adaxial ducts, 1.5 (0.6 to 2.6) and abaxial ducts, 3.9

(2.1 to 5.6) (confirmed by Deneke and Funsch 1972). This subspecies has fewest needles per fascicle, 2.4 (2.2 to 2.8) (not confirmed by Read 1980, studying 3-year-old seedlings).

Mature cones are ovoid to globose and have a form factor of 0.90 (0.8 to 1.0) (fig. 7). Proportional length of seed wing, as a multiple of seed length, is almost lowest for the species, 3.3 (3.2 to 3.5). Critchfield (1984) reported that pollen cones are red or purple.

Central High Plains ponderosa pine grows on breaks of the White, Niobrara, and Platte Rivers in western Nebraska and adjacent portions of South Dakota, Wyoming, and Colorado. It can be distinguished from adjacent Rocky Mountains ponderosa pine by several characteristics. Most notable about central plains ponderosa pine are foxtail-like foliage, extending almost twice as far along shoots; upright branching habit; fewer branches per whorl; 40-percent longer needles, much less appressed to the branch; more resin ducts in each needle; and more layers of hypoderm in corners of needles.

Read (1980) noted that needles on 3-year-old seedlings from his particular plots, that I would refer to subsp. *readiana*, were much longer (confirming my finding)

Figure 7—One selected cone from each of six trees, type of *Pinus ponderosa* subsp. *readiana*.

and much less appressed to stem than were those on seedlings of subsp. *scopulorum*. He also found that 3-year-old seedlings of subsp. *readiana* were taller and heavier than comparable seedlings of subsp. *scopulorum*. My examination of data published by Wells (1964) and Wright et al. (1969), for trees grown in Michigan, did not disclose any significant differences between the two subspecies.

5. *Pinus ponderosa* Douglas ex C. Lawson subsp. *brachyptera* (Engelm. in Wislizenus), *comb. nov.*, southwestern ponderosa pine—
Pinus brachyptera Engelm. in Wislizenus, Mem. Tour No. Mex., Senate Misc. Publ. 26, 30th U.S. Congr. 89. 1848.[30]—*Pinus ponderosa* var. *brachyptera* (Engelm. in Wislizenus) Lemmon, Second Biennial Rpt. Calif. State Board For. 73, 98. 1888.—

Type: " ... beginning about Rock creek[31] (sic) to Santa Fe" (specimen label; a highway distance of 63 miles, 101 km), "Mountains of New Mexico" (protologue); from journal by Wislizenus, I determined the type locality to be in San Miguel County, along Gallinas Creek, south of Las Vegas toward Romeroville, (probably T15N, R16E, NMB,[32] at 8,000 ft elev., approximate latitude 35°40' N, longitude 105°28' W) reported on 25 June 1846, specimen label dated 5 July 1846 (when the collector was in Santa Fe). Dr. A. Wislizenus s n. 534 (type: MO 1817026-27). Read's (1980) plot 864 is from this type locality.

This taxon, when originally described by Engelmann, was not given a common name. Lemmon (1889, 1890) called it southern yellow pine, a name subsequently confused with common names for other pines in southeastern United States. I believe Critchfield (1984) was first to apply the name southwestern ponderosa pine to this taxon. Peloquin (1984), following Critchfield's lead, also used this common name.

Southwestern ponderosa pine is distinguished from all others by having the thinnest needles; a seed (body) that is widest in relation to length, seed form factor 1.48 (1.30 to 1.60); and shortest absolute length of seed wing, 15.5 mm (15.1to 19.3). This last feature caused Engelmann to call it *brachyptera*, "short-winged." Subsequently, Lemmon (1888) erred when he wrote "This pine was so named by Dr. Engelmann, from a mistaken impression that the seed-wings were very short."

Another distinguishing feature of southwestern ponderosa pine, overlooked in the study by Callaham (2013), is the waxy bloom covering current shoots of many

---

[30] Xerographed copy of type specimen provided as in footnote 23.

[31] J. Richard Salazar, Chief, Archival Services, State Records, Santa Fe, New Mexico, in a March 8, 1995, conversation, said there is no "Rock Creek" in either San Miguel County or Santa Fe County. He cited his authority as Pearce (1965). Perhaps Wislizenus applied the name "Rock Creek" to the Gallinas River. Its bed is close to Romeroville where on June 25, 1846, he first described this pine in his journal.

[32] Same source as footnote 28, personal communication, August 21, 1991.

seedlings and trees. Its color has been described variously as "purple," "gray," or "white" (Read 1980, Weidman 1939, Wells 1964, Wright et al. 1969). A very high proportion of specimens from this subspecies, examined in the IFG herbarium in Placerville, California, had a whitish purple bloom on current shoots.

Other important characteristics that distinguish southwestern ponderosa pine are:

- Years needles stay green, 4.3 (2.5 to 5.9)
- Foliage length, 218 (66 to 538) mm
- Branches per whorl, 3.4 (1.6 to 6.6)
- Branch angle, 48 (30 to 79) degrees
- Needle length, 147 (112 to 198) mm
- Needles per fascicle, 3.0 (2.7 to 3.5)
- Hypodermal cell layers, 4.1 (3.4 to 4.5)
- Adaxial resin ducts per needle, 1.2 (0.7 to 2.4)
- Cone form, 0.86 (0.80 to 1.00)
- Seed plus wing length, 23.3 (18.2 to 26.2) mm.

Buds are grayish brown with closely appressed scales (Wright et al. 1969).

Monoterpenes in xylem oleoresin include a low but variable proportion of *delta*-3-carene (15 to 42 percent) and a moderate to high proportion of amount of *alpha*-pinene (38 to 50 percent); color of oleoresin exuding from xylem "is colorless to light amber" (Smith 1977).

Southwestern ponderosa pine differs significantly from adjacent Rocky Mountains ponderosa pine (table 1) by more consistently having three needles per fascicle (confirmed by Read 1980). Its needles are slightly narrower but 30 percent longer (confirmed by Read 1980). Its seeds are less elongate. Seed wings are nearly a millimeter shorter. Read (1980) also showed that its seedlings:

- Started growth much later
- Grew both faster and larger
- Had longer needles and needle sheaths
- Had divergent needles (that is, were less appressed)
- Tended to have shoots covered by a waxy bloom [confirmed by Wright et al. (1969)].

Smith (1977) showed that monoterpenes differ significantly with southwestern ponderosa pine having a relatively low proportion of *delta*-3-carene (15 to 42 vs. 37 to 55 percent) and a very high proportion of *alpha*-pinene (38 to 50 vs. 12 to 29 percent).

Significant differences from Pacific ponderosa pine were discussed previously under the section where that subspecies was described.

Acknowledgments

This paper was written and revised after consultations with Lawrence Heckard, then Curator of the Jepson Herbarium at the University of California at Berkeley, and John Strother, University Herbarium of the University of California at Berkeley. I am deeply indebted to them for the guidance and technical support they generously provided. Special appreciation is expressed to Dr. Strother for providing Latin diagnoses for new subspecies, examining specimens held in other herbaria, preparing and distributing to herbaria the specimens for new taxa, providing guidance on dealing with taxonomic difficulties, and contributing to improvements in the manuscript.

Friedrich Lauria, Department of Botany, Natural History Museum, Vienna, Austria—the world's leading authority on ponderosa pine—generously provided helpful comments on the manuscript, drafts of his publications in progress, his "Index to Nomenclature (Synonymy) of *Pinus ponderosa* and its Complex," findings from his studies in the United Kingdom, and reprints from what must be the most comprehensive collection of documents pertaining to taxonomy of ponderosa pine and related species.

This study was made possible, in part, by a grant from the Forest Genetics Research Foundation to the Institute of Forest Genetics, USDA Forest Service, Placerville, California.

Metric Equivalents

When you know:	Multiply by:	To find:
Feet (ft)	0.305	Meters
Miles (mi)	1.609	Kilometers

Literature Cited

Brayshaw, T.C. 1997. Washoe and ponderosa pines on Promontory Hill near Merritt, B.C., Canada. Wien, Austria: Annalen des Naturhistorischen Museums in Wien. 99B: 673–680.

Callaham, R.Z.; Liddicoet, A.R. 1961. Altitudinal variation at 20 years in ponderosa and Jeffrey pines. Journal of Forestry. 59(11): 814–820.

Callaham, R.Z. 2013. *Pinus ponderosa*: Geographic races and subspecies based on morphological variation. Res. Pap. PSW-RP-265. Albany, CA: U.S. Department of Agriculture, Forest Service, Pacific Southwest Research Station. 53 p.

Conkle, M.T. 1973. Growth data for 29 years from the California elevational transect study of ponderosa pine. Forest Science. 19(1): 31–39.

Conkle, M.T.; Critchfield, W.B. 1988. Genetic variation and hybridization of ponderosa pine. In: Baumgartner, D.M.; Lotan, J.E., eds. Proceedings, Symposium on ponderosa pine—the species and its management, Spokane, Washington, 27–43.

Coues, E. 1893. History of the expedition under the command of Lewis and Clark, Volume 1. New York: Francis P. Harper. 352 p.

Critchfield, W.B. 1984. Crossability and relationships of Washoe pine. Madroño. 31: 144–170.

Critchfield, W.B.; Allenbaugh, G.L. 1965. Washoe pine on the Bald Mountain Range, California. Madroño. 18: 63–64.

Critchfield, W.B.; Little, E.L. , Jr. 1966. Geographic distribution of the pines of the world. Misc. Pub. 991. Washington, DC: U.S. Department of Agriculture, Forest Service. 97 p.

Deneke, F.; Funsch, R.W. 1972. Resin canal number varies in ponderosa pine (*Pinus ponderosa* Laws.). Silvae Genetica. 21: 252.

Douglas, D. 1827. An account of a new species of Pinus, native of California: in a letter to Joseph Sabine, Esq., F.R. and L.S., Secretary of the Horticultural Society. Transactions of the Linnean Society of London. 15: 497–500.

Douglas, D. 1836. A sketch of a journey to the north-western parts of the continent of North America, during the years 1824, 5, 6, and 7. Comp. Bot. Mag. 2: 82–140.

Douglas, D. 1914. Journal kept by David Douglas during his travels in North America, 1823–1827. London: William Wesley and Son. 364 p.

Duffield, J.W. 1952. Relationships and species hybridization in the genus *Pinus*. Z. Forstg. u. Forstpflanzenz. Silvae Genetica. 1: 93–100.

Duffield, J.W.; Cumming, W.C. 1949. Does *Pinus ponderosa* occur in Baja California? Madroño. 10: 22–24.

Engelmann, G. 1848. Botanical appendix. In: Wislizenus, A., ed., Memoir of a tour to northern Mexico, connected with Col. Doniphan's expedition, in 1846 and 1847. Misc. Doc. 26. Washington, DC, 30th Congress, United States Senate: 89.

Engelmann, G. 1878. Coniferae. In: Report upon United States geographical surveys west of the one hundredth meridian, in charge of First Lieut. Geo. M. Wheeler. Vol. 6 Botany. Washington, DC: Government Printing Office.

Engelmann, G. 1879 [1880]. Tribe III. *Abietineae*. In: Watson, Sereno (ed.) Geological survey of California, botany. Cambridge, MA: University Press, John Wilson and Son. 2: 125–126.

Gordon, G. 1858. The pinetum: being a synopsis of all the coniferous plants at present known, with descriptions, history, and synonymies, and comprising nearly one hundred new kinds. Third issue, with additions. London: Henry G. Bohn: 202–203.

Gordon, G. 1862. A supplement to Gordon's pinetum: containing descriptions and additional synonymes of all the coniferous plants not before enumerated in that work with corrections up to the present time. London: Henry G. Bohn: 67.

Gottlieb, L. D. 1984. Genetic and morphological evolution in plants. American Naturalist. 123(5): 681–709.

Haller, J.R. 1961. Some recent observations on ponderosa, Jeffrey, and Washoe pines in northeastern California. Madroño. 16: 126–132.

Haller, J.R. 1962. Variation and hybridization in ponderosa and Jeffrey pine. University of California Publications in Botany. 34(2): 123–166.

Haller, J.R. 1965a. *Pinus washoensis* in Oregon: taxonomic and evolutionary implications. American Journal of Botany. 52: 646 (abst.).

Haller, J.R. 1965b. The role of 2-needle fascicles in the adaptation and evolution of ponderosa pine. Brittonia. 17(4): 354–382.

Haller, J.R.; Vivrette, N.J. 2011. Ponderosa pine revisited. Aliso. 29(1): 53–57.

Hartweg, T. 1847. Journal of a mission to California in search of plants. Part III. Journal of the Horticultural Society of London. 2: 187–191.

Hartweg, T. 1848. Journal of a mission to California in search of plants. Part IV. Journal of the Horticultural Society of London. 3: 217–228.

James, E.P. 1823. Account of an expedition from Pittsburgh to the Rocky Mountains, performed in the years 1819 and '20, by order of the Hon. J. C. Calhoun, Sec'y of War; under the command of Major Stephen H. Long. From the notes of Major Long, Mr. T. Say, and other gentlemen of the exploring party. Compiled by Edwin James, botanist and geologist for the expedition. Philadelphia, PA: American Philatelic Society. 2 vol., Atlas.

James, E.P. 1825. Catalogue of plants collected during a journey to and from the Rocky Mountains, during the summer of 1820. Philadelphia, PA: Transactions of the American Philosophical Society, New Series. 2(8): 172–190.

Kempff, G. 1928. Non-indigenous western yellow pine plantations in northern Idaho. Northwest Science. 2(2): 54–58.

LaFarge, T. 1974. Genetic differences in stem form of ponderosa pine grown in Michigan. Silvae Genetica. 23: 211–213.

Larson, M.M. 1967. Effect of temperature on initial development of ponderosa pine seedlings from three sources. Forest Science. 13(3): 286–294.

Lauria, F. 1991. Taxonomy, systematics, and phylogeny of *Pinus*, subsection *Ponderosae* Loudon (Pinaceae). Alternative concepts. Linzer Biologische Beitraege. 23(1): 129–202.

Lauria, F. 1996. The identity of *Pinus ponderosa* Douglas ex C Lawson (Pinaceae). Linzer Biologische Beitraege. 28(2): 999–1052.

Lauria, F. 1997. The taxonomic status of *Pinus washoensis* H. Mason & Stockw. (Pinaceae). Annalen des Naturhistorischen Museums in Wien. 99B: 655–671.

Lawson, C. (P. Lawson and Son.) 1836. The agriculturist's manual: being a familiar description of the agricultural plants cultivated in Europe. Edinburgh, United Kingdom: William Blackwood and Sons, 430 p.

Lemmon, J.G. 1888. Pines of the Pacific slope. In: Second biennial report of the California State Board of Forestry for the years 1887–1888. Sacramento, CA: State Board of Forestry: 73: 97–99.

Lemmon, J.G. 1889. Supplement to forestry report for 1887 and 1888—Botanist's Department. Revision of broken-cone pines. Sacramento, CA: California State Board of Forestry Bul. 7: 6–11.

Lemmon, J.G. 1890. Revision of broken-cone pines. In: Third Biennial Report, California State Board of Forestry for the years 1889–1890. Sacramento, CA: California State Board of Forestry: 196–201.

Lemmon, J.G. 1893. Notes on west American Coniferae.–II. Erythia. 1: 134–136.

Lemmon, J.G. 1895. Handbook of west–American conebearers. 3rd ed. Privately published, Oakland, CA. p. 35.

Lemmon, J.G. 1897. Three west-American conifers. Garden and Forest. 10: 183.

Lemmon, J.G. 1900. Handbook of west–American conebearers. 4th (pocket) ed. Privately published, Oakland, CA.

Linhart, Y.B.; Grant, M.C.; Montazer, P. 1989. Experimental studies in ponderosa pine. I. Relationship between variation in proteins and morphology. American Journal of Botany. 76(7): 1024–1032.

Little, E.L., Jr. 1971. Atlas of United States trees. Vol. 1. Conifers and important hardwoods. Misc. Pub. 1146. Washington, DC: U.S. Department of Agriculture, Forest Service. 200 p.

Little, E.L., Jr. 1979. Checklist of United States trees (native and naturalized.) Agric. Handb. 541. Washington, DC: U.S. Department of Agriculture, Forest Service. 375 p.

Little, E.L., Jr.; Critchfield, W.B. 1969. Subdivisions of the genus *Pinus* (pines). Misc. Pub. 1144. Washington, DC: U.S. Department of Agriculture, Forest Service. 51 p.

Loudon, J.C. 1830. Hortus Britannicus. London: Longman, Rees, Orme, Brown and Green. 576 p.

Manetti, J. 1844. Catalogi plantarum, caesarei regii horti, prope modiciam, supplementum primum. Mediolani. 28 p.

Mason, H.L.; Stockwell, P. 1945. A new pine from Mount Rose, Nevada. Madroño. 8(2): 61–63.

McKelvey, S.D. 1955. Botanical exploration of the trans-Mississippi west, 1790–1850. Jamaica Plains, MA: Arnold Arboretum of Harvard University: 957.

Mirov, N.T. 1929. Chemical analysis of the oleoresins as a means of distinguishing Jeffrey pine and western yellow pine. Journal of Forestry. 27: 176–187.

Mirov, N.T. 1961. Composition of gum turpentines of pines. Tech. Bull. 1239. Washington, DC: U.S. Department of Agriculture. 158 p.

Moore, M.B.; Kidd, F.A. 1982. Seed source variation in induced moisture stress germination of ponderosa pine. Tree Planters' Notes. 33(l): 12–14.

Murray, A. 1855. Description of new coniferous trees from California. Edinburgh New Philosophical Journal. Series 2. 1: 284–295.

Murray, E. 1982. Notae Spermatophytae. Kalmia. 12: 23. July.

Niebling, C.R.; Conkle, M.T. 1990. Diversity of Washoe pine and comparisons with allozymes of ponderosa pine races. Canadian Journal of Forest Research. 20: 298–308.

Pearce, T.M. 1965. New Mexico place names. Albuquerque, NM: University of New Mexico Press.

Peloquin, R.L. 1984. The identification of three-species hybrids in the ponderosa pine complex. The Southwestern Naturalist. 29(1): 115–122.

Perry, J.P., Jr. 1991. The pines of Mexico and Central America. Portland, OR: Timber Press. 231 p.

Read, R.A. 1980. Genetic variation in seedling progeny of ponderosa pine provenances. Forest Science. Monograph 23. 59 p.

Read, R.A. 1983. Ten-year performance of ponderosa pine provenances in the Great Plains of North America. Res. Pap. RM-RP-250. Fort Collins, CO: U.S. Department of Agriculture, Forest Service, Rocky Mountain Forest and Range Experiment Station. 17 p.

Read. R.A.; Sprackling, J.A.. 1981. Hail damage variation by seed source in a ponderosa pine plantation. Res. Note RM-RN-410. Fort Collins, CO: U.S. Department of Agriculture, Forest Service, Rocky Mountain Forest and Range Experiment Station. 6 p.

Rehfeldt, G.E. 1986a. Adaptive variation in *Pinus ponderosa* from Intermountain regions. I. Middle Columbia River system. Res. Pap. INT-RP-373. Ogden, UT: U.S. Department of Agriculture, Forest Service, Intermountain Research Station. 9 p.

Rehfeldt, G.E. 1986b. Adaptive variation in *Pinus ponderosa* from Intermountain regions. II. Snake and Salmon River basins. Forest Science. 32: 79–92.

Rehfeldt, G.E. 1990. Genetic differentiation among populations of *Pinus ponderosa* from the upper Colorado River basin. Botanical Gazette. 151: 125–137.

Rehfeldt, G.E. 1991. Models of genetic variation for *Pinus ponderosa* in the inland Northwest (U.S.A.). Canadian Journal of Forest Research. 21: 1491–1500.

Rehfeldt, G.E. 1993. Genetic variation in the *Ponderosae* of the Southwest. American Journal of Botany. 80: 330–343.

Rehfeldt, G.E.; Wilson, B.C.;Wilson, S.P.; Jeffers, R.M. 1996. Phytogeographic, taxonomic, and genetic implications of phenotypic variation in the *Ponderosae* of the Southwest. The Southwestern Naturalist. 41(4): 409–418.

Rehfeldt, G.E. 1999a. Systematics and genetic structure of Washoe pine: Applications to conservation genetics. Silvae Genetica 48(3–4): 167–173.

Rehfeldt, G.E. 1999b. Systematics and genetic structure of *Ponderosae* taxa (Pinaceae) inhabiting the mountain islands of the Southwest. American Journal of Botany. 86: 741–752.

Righter, F.I.; Duffield, J.W. 1951. Interspecies hybrids in pines. Journal of Heredity. 42: 75–80.

Sargent, C.S. 1889. Notes upon some North American trees. Garden and Forest. 2: 496.

Sargent, C.S. 1897. The first account of some western trees. Garden and Forest. 10: 28, 29, 38–40.

Sargent, C. 1898. The silva of North America. Vol. 8. Coniferae. Boston and New York: Houghton, Mifflin and Co . p. 77–82. Reprinted in 7 vol., Vol. 7. Coniferae. 1947. New York: Peter Smith.

Shaw, G.R. 1909. The pines of Mexico. Publications of the Arnold Arboretum 1. Jamaica Plains, MA: Arnold Arboretum of Harvard University. 29 p.

Shaw, G.R. 1914. The genus *Pinus*. Publications of the Arnold Arboretum 5. Cambridge, MA: Riverside Press. 96 p.

Silba, J. 1990. A supplement to the international census of the Coniferae, II. Phytologia. 68(1): 59.

Smith, R.H. 1967. Variations in the monoterpene composition of the wood resin of Jeffrey, Washoe, Coulter and lodgepole pines. Forest Science. 13: 246–252.

Smith, R.H. 1971. Xylem monoterpenes of *Pinus ponderosa*, *P. washoensis*, and *P. jeffreyi* in the Warner Mountains of California. Madroño. 21: 26–32.

Smith, R.H. 1977. Monoterpenes of ponderosa pine xylem resin in western United States. Tech. Bul. 1532. Washington, DC: U.S. Department of Agriculture, Forest Service. 48 p.

Sorenson, F.C., Mandel, N.L.; Aagaard, J.E. 2001. Role of selection versus historical isolation in racial differentiation of ponderosa pine in southern Oregon: an investigation of alternative hypotheses. Canadian Journal of Forest Research. 31: 1127–1139.

Sudworth, G.B. 1897. Nomenclature of the arborescent flora of the United States. Bulletin 14. Washington, DC: U.S. Department of Agriculture, Division of Forestry. 419 p.

Ting, W.S. 1966. Determination of Pinus species by pollen statistics. University of California Publications in Geological Sciences. 58: 116.

Torrey, J. 1828. Some account of a collection of plants made during a journey to and from the Rocky Mountains in the summer of 1820, by Edwin P. James, M.D., Assistant Surgeon, U.S. Army. New York: Annals of the Lyceum of Natural History of New York. 2: 161–254.

Van Haverbake, D.F. 1988. Genetic variation in ponderosa pine: a 15-year test of provenances in the Great Plains. Res. Pap. RM-RP-265. Fort Collins, CO: U.S. Department of Agriculture, Forest Service, Rocky Mountain Forest and Range Experiment Station. 16 p.

Vasey, G. 1876. Catalog of the forest trees of the United States. Washington, DC: Government Printing Office. 38 p.

Wang, Chi-Wu. 1977. Genetics of ponderosa pine. Res. Pap. WO–34. Washington, DC: U.S. Department of Agriculture, Forest Service. 24 p.

Wells, O.O. 1964. Geographic variation in ponderosa pine. I. The ecotypes and their distribution. Silvae Genetica. 13(4): 89–103.

Weidman, R.H. 1939. Evidences of racial influence in a 25-year test of ponderosa pine. Journal of Agricultural Research. 59(12): 855–887.

Wislizenus, A. 1848. Memoir of a tour to northern Mexico connected with Col. Doniphan's expedition, in 1846 and 1847. Senate Misc. Doc. 26. Washington, DC: 30th Session.

Wright, J.W.; Lemmien, W.A.; Bright, J.N. 1969. Early growth of ponderosa pine ecotypes in Michigan. Forest Science. 15(2): 121–129.